DERRY
DANCE HALLS OF ROMANCE

GUILDHALL PRESS

WILLIE DEERY

Published in November 2011

GUILDHALL PRESS
Unit 15, Ráth Mór Business Park
Bligh's Lane
Derry BT48 0LZ
Ireland
T: (00 44 28) 7136 4413
E: info@ghpress.com • W: www.ghpress.com

The author/photographers assert their moral rights in this work in accordance with the
Copyright, Designs and Patents Act 1998.

Design/Typesetting by Kevin Hippsley/Guildhall Press
Copyright © Willie Deery/Guildhall Press

ISBN: 978 1 906271 41 1
A CIP record for this book is available from the British Library.

Guildhall Press is grateful to Derry City Council
for Service Level Agreement support under the
remit of the Heritage and Museum Service.

Guildhall Press gratefully acknowledges the financial
support of the Arts Council of Northern Ireland
as a principal funder under its Annual Support for
Organisations Programme.

My Thanks To . . .

During my dander down memory lane for this publication I received lots of help from many people. Unfortunately, space doesn't permit me to name them all. But I would like to thank, and give special mention to, the following who freely contributed their photographs, time and knowledge with much encouragement:

Brian Flanagan (the Plaza, Buncrana), Robert Ferris, Colum Arbuckle, Isabel Doherty, Clare Bridge, Mary Clifford, Joe McCallion, Sean Coyle, Tony Quigley, Neilly McCarron, Roy Arbuckle, Bob and Belle Redmond (USA), Dave and Margaret Bland (USA), *Derry Journal*, LibrariesNI, John Gillespie, Sadie Gallagher, Ginger Doherty, Jimmy Kelly, Gerry Finneran, George Hasson, Willie Bradley, Billy Tyson, John Baird, Masie Crawford, Charlie Large, Paddy 'Beatle' McLaughlin, Jackie and Maureen McCauley, Brian Heaney, Pat MacCafferty, Danny and Frances McNally, Tommy Donnelly, Phil Cunningham, Micky McGuinness, Eamonn Melaugh, Barney McMonagle, the Willie Carson Collection, Patrick Durnin, Hugh Gallagher, Liam Reilly, Ernie Falconer and Frankie McMenamin.

I only hope I have done you all justice and that enjoying these great stories and wonderful images is some small reward for your invaluable help.

A final thank you to all at Guildhall Press whose hard work, creativity and good humour made putting this all together another fun experience: Declan, Kevin, Joe, Paul and Jenni.

Safe home!

Contents

ADMIT 1

Contents

ADMIT 1

Introduction

In the mid-1950s, Rock & Roll burst onto the scene in Ireland with a bang and was shortly followed by the showband explosion that took the country by storm.

These two innovations were to change the landscape of the Irish music-entertainment industry forever.

Many Derry people of that era enthuse it was a great time to be young, as entertainment options were plentiful. Along with several quality picture houses, the city and North West boasted great dance venues such as the Corinthian, Memorial Hall, Criterion, Guildhall, Embassy, Cameo/Stardust, Borderland, Pallidrome, Fiesta, Plaza and the Castle, all hosting top-class showbands on an almost nightly basis. The very mention of these dance halls today still brings a smile to anyone who spent their youth waltzing or jiving on their highly polished floors.

Promoters took advantage of the popularity of the emerging showbands and across Ireland, many hastily built buildings, some with just four walls and a tin roof, duly opened as ballrooms. Despite their primitive nature, these venues, too, became magnets for teenagers looking for adventure and to meet the partner of their dreams.

On the big-band scene, again Derry and the North West had much to be proud of with performers such as Johnny Quigley's All Stars, the Clipper Carlton, the Woodchoppers, James MacCafferty's Carlton Swingtette with Mick McWilliams, and arguably the most gifted musician this city has produced – Gay McIntyre with his band. Then along came the super-confident southern-based showmen of the Miami, the Royal, the Drifters and the Cadets who took it all to another level until the demise of this unique musical revolution in the mid-1970s.

Yours Truly and thousands of others travelled far and wide to the alcohol-free dances by every means of conveyance that was available including bicycle, bus and even tractor! Once there, we danced and romanced, rocked and rolled, and had the time of our lives. I have tried to capture here the magic moments of those carefree dance-hall days and the showbands who brought them alive with their music and their energy. I have also recalled some of the many couples who first met in the dance halls and the antics of some local Derry characters in what is a light-hearted, nostalgic trip down memory lane.

While researching for this book, I was delighted at the willingness of all those I approached to talk openly, and with much humour at times, about their experiences of those great dancing days. This is, in many ways, their story, too.

It is impossible in such limited space to mention, or do justice to, all the talented musicians and singers from across Ireland who entertained us back then in our youthful wonder years.

I hope they, and you, will overlook any discrepancies or omissions in this labour of love and sit back and enjoy one last visit to the Ballrooms of Romance.

Yours Truly
Willie Deery

Roller-skating at the famous Ashfield Hall in the 1940s. The Ashfield was one of the most popular dance halls of the 1930s and '40s.

Adverts from the Derry Journal of 1954 and 1956.

Dancing Days and Teenage Kicks

As parents and grandparents, there are times when we reminisce about the days of our youth. And when in a quiet and reflective mood, we tend to compare the lifestyle of the youth of today with our own of days gone by. Looking back on the changing trends of how the young ones of different generations enjoyed their social lives makes the mind boggle. For instance, it is fair to say that we believe, rightly or wrongly, that the social life of today's young people is, by nature, spontaneous, unplanned and occasionally thoughtless. This may be true to an extent, simply because a lot of today's young people have cars and can go where and when they choose on the spur of the moment, whereas back in the 1950s, '60s and '70s, we believed we had a more planned style to our social lives – with perhaps only the miniskirt surviving the test of time!

We also tend to highlight the shortcomings of today's youth when comparing them with the youth of our own generation. But in truth, is it not the case that maybe our minds play tricks on us? Could it not be that our fading memories tend to erase our own shortcomings? Maybe in the same way we seem to forget about the bad weather that existed in the '50s and '60s? Cast aside from our minds and seemingly forever from our memories are the dark, cold, wet and dreary days that really did exist when we were young, with perhaps only the long, sun-drenched, carefree days of summer allowed to remain in our minds. Is it not also fair comment to suggest that the boys and men of yesteryear also did their fair share of drinking? Not so much so, however, for the girls and women of that time when such things were frowned upon for them.

However, being a teenager back then was undoubtedly much different to being one in today's world. Some of the obvious differences were, even though we may have been working, we still didn't have much pocket money, simply because on receiving our weekly pay packet, it was the done thing to hand over more than half of it to our mothers. Also, the clothes we wore going to a dance could have been borrowed from our friends, as swapping clothes was the norm back then. And, of

11

course, those were the days when bathing in many homes was courtesy of the tin bath or enamel basin and the only water tap was situated in the back yard. Not to mention that only tea and lemonade were allowed to be sold in the dance halls.

Although these contrasting lifestyle differences were certainly stark, perhaps the most distinct difference was in how we were entertained on our nights 'out the town'. Unlike today's teenagers, who now mostly dance to a disc jockey playing records, we had not one, but two live bands to entertain us, one of which was an eight- or nine-piece showband, and both playing live music. We also went dancing in larger numbers and much more frequently than the young of today, as dances then were held on an almost nightly basis.

But back then, it wasn't just viewed as a dance; it was much more than that. It was a social event and the highlight of our week. The dance halls were a place where people from every background came together, not only to dance and be entertained, but in the real hope of meeting the man or woman of their dreams who maybe would become their partner for life. Just as it is today, that first contact was always the hardest to make, but somehow it felt a lot easier back then.

In our early days, we would travel miles to attend the alcohol-free dances. We came from the cities, from the country and down from the hills. We travelled by all means of conveyance: bus, minibus, taxi, motorbike, push-bike and even by tractor. We crowded into cars; three in the front and five in the back. And if we couldn't organise a lift, we just started walking and hitch-hiked our way there. We descended in droves to every city or small village that had a dance hall. And we queued in orderly fashion to pay our 5/- (25p), 7/6d (37p) or ten bob (50p) entrance fee.

When we walked through the doors of a dance hall we would feel not only the heat but the atmosphere, which was simply electric. And there was what we now call the 'feel-good factor' in abundance, with hundreds of people from all walks of life on the dance floor enjoying themselves. The whole experience was so infectious; there were smiling faces all around you … even if it was only the relief band on stage at that time!

By the time the big band took to the stage, the people who had been drinking in the nearby pubs would be in the dance hall and the whole place would be buzzing. The crowds were so big, all that could be seen on the dance floor was a sea of heads moving to the beat of the big showband. If you saw a space suddenly developing on the crowded floor then you knew there was probably a fight taking place! But then again, that was normal, too … because it was a showband dance.

During the night, such were the crowds that if you went out dancing with a girl after that particular set was over, it was at times difficult to find your mates again. If you were leaving a girl home, it was a great relief if you could get her to the mineral bar to buy her a soft drink. The heat in the dance halls was such that your clothes were stuck to your skin by your own sweat. What a feeling! What a time to be young! Teenage kicks hit us long before the Undertones were to experience theirs.

St Columb's Hall functioned as a picture house and a concert hall.

That's Entertainment

In the 1950s, Derry was a remarkable place to live as families were only just coming out of post-war poverty. For the first time in God knows how long, people had a few shillings in their pockets. Some were to experience the comfort of a new suit, shirt or dress on their back for the very first time.

After a hard week working in the factories, building sites, shops or offices, the dance halls became the focal point of our expectations. On a Friday, the *Derry Journal* entertainment pages were scoured from corner to corner to see what bands were playing that Friday, Saturday or Sunday night. In Derry back then, the dance halls – along with the six picture houses – provided the main entertainment for the young people.

Actually, it was the in-thing to take a girl to the pictures on a first date after leaving her home from a dance at the weekend. If she agreed to go to the Monday-night pictures with you everyone classed you as being practically engaged! The worst part of going to the pictures with a girl was the inevitable slagging you had to take from your mates if they happened to be at the same show. There was nothing as embarrassing as being caught carrying a bag of sweets with a girl linked on to your arm on that first date. The local picture houses going at the time were the Rialto, the Strand, the Palace, the City, St Columb's Hall, and the sole premises in the Waterside, the Midland. All did a roaring trade in those days and we certainly lacked no shortage of entertainment options back then.

Venues old and new. The Rialto in foreground with the Millennium Forum under construction in the background.

The City Cinema in William Street.

CITY CINEMA Continuous from 2.15

To-morrow, Fri., Sat.: Leo Gorcey and the Bowery Boys, **Hard-boiled Mahoney** 2.30, 4.55, 7.15, 9.40
Kirby Grant in **Fangs of the Antarctic** 3.35, 6.00, 8.25

To-night: **The Naked Spur**; also **Air Raid Wardens**

PALACE Cinema Continuous from 2.00

ALL WEEK:

Charlton Heston, Nicole Murray and Robert Young in

Secret of the Incas

(Technicolor) — 2.30, 4.40, 6.50, 9.05

Midland
Phone 2740
Balcony 1/8
Back Stalls .. 1/-
Front Stalls .. 9d

— MATINEE DAILY AT 3.00 p.m. —

To-day:
STERLING HAYDEN and GLORIA GRAHAME in
NAKED ALIBI

To-morrow, Fri., Sat.:
Duncan Macrae, Adrienne Corri, Vincent Winter in
The Kidnappers

The Midland Cinema in Bond's Hill.

The Palace Cinema in Shipquay Street.

The Strand Cinema on the Strand Road.

The clock on the wall reads 12.29am, the year 1949, the place, the Corinthian Ballroom in Bishop Street. This dance is in full swing as resident band the Carlton Swingtette belts out the music. Included: Barney Coyle, Willie 'The Pope' Gallagher, Peter McLaughlin, Mick McWilliams and band leader James MacCafferty.

The main dance halls in Derry then were the Corinthian, the Capitol (later to become the Embassy), the Criterion, Memorial Hall (Mem), the Clarendon and Ritz halls and Derry's Guildhall. In the country areas outside the city, there were many Orange Halls that also held weekly dances. These ballrooms followed on from the likes of the Melville, Oaks and Ashfield dance halls of the 1940s. The Derry ballrooms had it all to themselves for years, and sell-out crowds were the norm at each venue. However, their dominance came to an end when, on Wednesday 15 December 1954, the Borderland Ballroom, situated just over the border in the village of Muff in County Donegal, opened its doors for the first time.

The first band to play in what was arguably the most popular dance venue of that era in or around Derry was the Flying Carlton Dance Band from Dundalk. Compére for this memorable opening night was Eddie O'Doherty and admission was a whopping ten shillings. Dancing, which lasted a marathon six hours, was from 9.00pm to 3.00am. Several hundred people were turned away from the doors on that first night as the hall was packed to capacity within thirty minutes of the doors opening. Special buses left from Great James Street in Derry at 9.30pm, returning immediately after the dance. These buses were to become the main conveyances to and from Borderland for Derry dancers for years to come.

GRAND
Opening Dance
— IN —
The Borderland Ballroom
(IRELAND'S LATEST LUXURY BALLROOM)
-- **Muff** --
WEDNESDAY NEXT, 15th DEC.
MUSIC BY:
The Flying Carlton Dance Band
COMPERE — EDDIE O'DOHERTY
VALUABLE SPOT PRIZES • Dancing • MODERN SNACK BAR. TEAS.
GOLD WATCHES, etc. 9 to 3 COFFEE, CAKES, etc.
Admission — Ten Shillings. | Dress Optional.
BUSES leave Great James Street, Derry, at 9.30 p.m., returning immediately after the dance.
RIGHT OF ADMISSION STRICTLY RESERVED

The Clipper Carlton Light the Fuse

In the 1950s and '60s, the main employment opportunities for women and girls in Derry were the many shirt factories that existed; the BSR factory on Bligh's Lane was the main employer for the men and teenage boys. Other places of employment were the building sites, Du Pont, Browns Foundry, Lipton's, Woolworth's, Littlewoods, the All Cash Stores, some family-run clothes shops and different offices throughout Derry. Even with those workplaces, while female employment was plentiful, male unemployment was still very high. There were many showbands in Derry which offered musicians good money for part-time employment, but many mothers didn't consider playing in a band a normal job for their sons. In fact, there was an old saying among mothers when asked was their musician son working and the reply would be, 'No, he's not working; he's playing in a showband.' With

After a hard week's work in the Star Factory, workers looked forward to a weekend of dancing. Taking a tea break in 1958 are Annie McAnaney, Gerry White, Sheila Clarke, Josie Kelpie (later to marry Noel Crampsey) and Betty McLaughlin.

Dancing shoes going cheap at MacLaughlin's shop in Waterloo Street in 1956.

Dancers waltzing to the Woodchoppers in the 1950s in the old Plaza, Buncrana. This hall would later become the café when the new Plaza Ballroom was built adjoining it several years later.

money being obviously scarce, the pawnshops of Barr's, Arthur's and Crossan's were still needed in emergencies and did a roaring trade in those days.

At that particular time, there was an air of innocence among the dancers, as at each dance the same pattern would emerge. The girls would arrive early and take up positions at one side of the dance hall. The men, some slightly intoxicated, would arrive later and stand on the opposite side of the floor, like sprinters waiting for the starting gun to go off, their eyes fixed to the female side of the hall, all waiting for someone else to make the first move. Men were reluctant to be the first across the floor for fear of refusal by the girl, because if that happened, it was a long walk back to the male side of the hall and all eyes would be fixed on him. This embarrassing rejection would normally spoil the man's night. However, once the first man made his move, there would follow a near stampede by the men towards the women of their choice to ask them to dance.

In the early 1950s, cheek-to-cheek contact with your partner was considered unacceptable behaviour and was not permitted on the dance floor. If a couple became a little too amorous and were dancing too close, they would be gently tapped on the shoulder by a bouncer and told to cool it. Also, jiving was frowned upon by the dance-hall owners and only permitted in one corner at the rear of a ballroom, simply because they considered jiving was not proper dancing and took up too much space on the dance floor. And it hindered the 'proper' dancers who waltzed their way in the same direction around the waxed dance floor.

The musicians of that era were also of a more refined nature. They dressed in tuxedo, white shirt and bow tie, were seated on stage and read from music sheets on stands. Back then, everyone would dance the night away to a near orchestra on stage, as the bands had an average of about a dozen members.

A big hit with the dancers in the 1950s was the very popular Stan Cauley Orchestra. Pictured are Jim McDermott, Paddy Boyle, Brendan Clifford, Stan at the piano, Noel Lindsay, Jimmy 'China Doll' Liddy, Hugh 'Crazy Man' Griffiths and Peter McLaughlin.

This stiff-collar approach was resigned to the dustbin in the mid-1950s when eight young musicians from Strabane called the Clipper Carlton changed the music scene in Ireland forever. How did they do this? Simply by discarding their chairs and music stands and performing standing up. And not only did they play on their feet all night but they now moved to the rhythm of their music.

The men who changed the band scene in Ireland forever, the famous and incomparable Clipper Carlton from Strabane, in Borderland, 1962.

The Blue Notes in the mid-1950s: J McDermott, N Lindsay, J Liddy, B Clifford, P Boyle, L Fullock, P McLaughlin and H Griffiths.

This new development by the Strabane band was greeted with enthusiasm by the dancers, who simply loved it. Word travelled around the country about this new craze, and soon other bands throughout Ireland followed the style set by the Clipper Carlton. They put the 'show' into the bands' performances, and now all the bands became showbands. The Clipper Carlton was credited, and rightly so, with lighting the fuse that led to the showband explosion countrywide in the late 1950s and the 1960s. The Clipper Carlton Saturday Night Juke-Box Show set the scene for the start of a never-to-be-forgotten era in Irish entertainment and dances.

At that particular time, they were by far the biggest attraction in Ireland, north or south. The location of the venue didn't matter – Derry, Belfast, Dublin, Cork or some remote village in rural Ireland – the result was the same: packed dance halls with sell-out crowds. They were a great influence on other showbands starting out on the road and on up-and-coming young entertainers the length and breadth of Ireland. One such entertainer was young Waterford singer, Brendan Bowyer.

Brendan, later of the famed Royal Showband, had this to say about the Clipper Carlton. 'I was a young teenager and at that time I was particularly influenced by the Clipper Carlton Showband from Strabane. I remember it being my summer holidays from school in 1956 that I first heard the Clippers. I was utterly stunned by their talent and versatility … and they were standing up! Remember, all dance bands at that time were sitting down while playing their instruments. For an impressionable sixteen-year-old, this was pure magic. I can now honestly say this was a defining moment in my life, and that experience inspired me to be a professional entertainer.'

It is undeniable that the Clipper Carlton was the catalyst that created the showband phenomenon in Ireland. However, the first band to use the term 'showband' was Derry's Willie Campbell Showband when they were advertised as such in the *Derry Journal* of Friday 10 December 1954 for a dance in Derry's Guildhall.

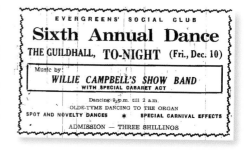

EVERGREENS' SOCIAL CLUB

Sixth Annual Dance

THE GUILDHALL, TO-NIGHT (Fri., Dec. 10)

Music by

WILLIE CAMPBELL'S SHOW BAND
WITH SPECIAL CABARET ACT

Dancing 9 p.m. till 2 a.m.
OLDE-TYME DANCING TO THE ORGAN
SPOT AND NOVELTY DANCES * SPECIAL CARNIVAL EFFECTS
ADMISSION — THREE SHILLINGS

Skiffle Bands and Harmony Groups

Another popular type of band appeared on the Derry scene in the mid-1950s when Pat McCrossan (snr) set up what is widely regarded as one of Derry's first skiffle groups in 1956. Pat called the group the Truckers and their signature tune was *Truck Driving Man*. They produced an extraordinary sound, different from most bands at the time, as it incorporated a washboard as one of its instruments. Of course, the skiffle groups were made popular by the famous Lonnie Donegan.

In the Truckers' first line-up were Pat McCrossan on washboard and fiddle, Seán Canning played upright bass, Seán Coyle was on guitar and vocals, and Charlie Coyle on guitar and vocal harmony. They had a regular spot with Josie McIntyre's Embassy Orchestra in the old Embassy Ballroom in the late 1950s. They also appeared in many concerts, notably at the famed St Columb's Hall. But good as skiffle was, it was no match for the massively popular showband sound.

With male unemployment very high, men found lots of ways to pass the time of day or night. Some walked greyhounds and others just met at street corners, where many a tall tale was told. Other forms of alternative entertainment sprang up, like harmony groups, with perhaps Pat and his Saddle Pals being one of the better-known ones. They played in many venues in Derry and became locally famous; they specialised in close harmonies and provided endless hours of free entertainment for the locals. That was back in the days when Derry had many a harmony group who passed the night away singing. Actually, it's widely believed that unemployment and street-corner groups were the reasons why Derry provided so many talented singers in those days.

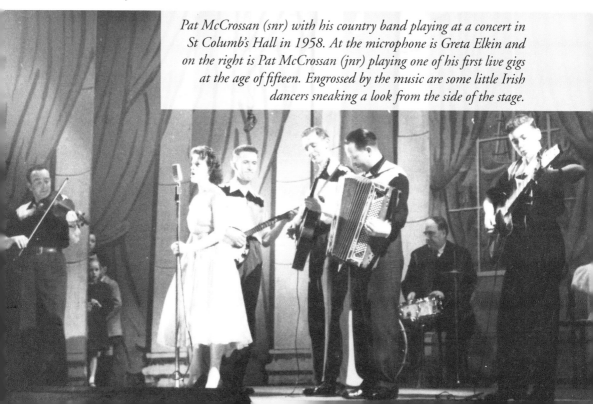

Pat McCrossan (snr) with his country band playing at a concert in St Columb's Hall in 1958. At the microphone is Greta Elkin and on the right is Pat McCrossan (jnr) playing one of his first live gigs at the age of fifteen. Engrossed by the music are some little Irish dancers sneaking a look from the side of the stage.

Roddy's Hotel (c.1900s) in Bishop Street, which later became famous as the Corinthian Ballroom.

The Corinthian: Derry's Most Popular Dance Hall

The Corinthian Ballroom was arguably the most popular dance hall in Derry City in the 1940s, '50s, and early '60s. Dancing was held at the Bishop Street venue close to the Diamond on Mondays, Wednesdays, Fridays and Saturdays, and the list of local bands and orchestras that played there is almost as long as the River Foyle! Every dancer could argue the merits of their own favourite band, but most would agree on one thing: how much they all enjoyed one dance in particular – Around the House. This was when the band played different tunes and different tempos, and the patrons danced the waltz, quickstep, slow foxtrot, tango, samba and a Gay Gordon – all in the one set!

The Woodchoppers at the Criterion Ballroom in 1958. Musicians include: Jackie Bonnar, Willie Bradley and Dickie McManus.

Maisie Crawford (née McNulty) from Alexander Place remembers dancing to popular songs of that era. 'The songs were lovely and melodic then, songs like *Cherry Pink and Apple Blossom Wine, Stranger In Paradise, Mona Lisa, Mr Sandman* and *Begin The Beguine*. They were very romantic tunes, and to tell you the truth, a girl would be raging if she didn't get lifted (asked to dance by a boy) when the band were playing such songs. Some of the men back then were awful shy, especially when they were sober. I loved dancing, and on a Monday night, when I could, I would have the wains washed, fed and in bed early. I would get myself all dolled up and wait patiently for my husband Walter to come back from the Paradiso Bar where he was playing darts to take me to the Memorial Hall.

Maisie Crawford waiting for husband Walter to return from playing darts in the Paradiso to take her to the Mem.

'This photograph of me (right) was taken on one such Monday night in 1963. I loved dancing and started going to the Mem when I was fourteen years old. The last quickstep was always *Cherry Pink and Apple Blossom Wine* and the last waltz would be *Brahms Lullaby*. When I hear *Brahms Lullaby* today I instantly think of waltzing around the Memorial Hall, which was on on Monday and Saturday nights. I remember 'Joker' Finlay was a regular playing there. Tuesday was the Crit and jiving to the Woodchoppers and Wednesday night the Corinthian, where you danced to the lovely voice of Mick McWilliams. The memories flood back to me when I think of those wonderful days of the '50s and '60s, memories that will never fade.'

Another person who was very active on the dance floor then was Neilly McCarron. Three incidents in particular come to his mind readily. The first one was the first time he dated his wife, Jean Moran, after meeting her in the Guildhall. Neilly explained: 'I was working up the courage to ask her out for weeks, but this night I was waiting no longer. After several dances with her, and weeks of rehearsing what to say to her, I finally asked off with her. She agreed to let me walk her home and that was the start of it. That was forty-six years ago. And there she is and here I am,' he laughs, looking at Jean sitting opposite him in their comfortable living room.

Another night from his youth which is etched in his mind was the night he and his mates robbed their pal of his coat to get the money for a dance in the Corinthian.

Neilly continues: 'I had a date with Jean, whom I was to see inside the Corinthian. But I had a problem; I was skint and so were my mates. It was a Wednesday and we tried everywhere to get a loan of a few bob to go to the dance but failed to do so. One of our mates, Robin Matchett, had just got a new overcoat, and he was wearing it for the first time that day. We asked him to pawn it so we could get the money we needed and we promised we would get it out again on Friday. He wouldn't hear tell of it and refused point-blank. We were now in dire straits, so again we asked him – no, *begged* him – to pawn his coat. Again he refused, saying his mother would go mad if he returned home without it.

'Well, as we all know, desperate situations cause people to do desperate things. We were standing in the snooker hall, racking our brains as to how we could get the money for the dance. We got a free game of snooker, so Robin took off his overcoat and hung it up on the rail. Mike McAllister, who also had a date with his girlfriend that night, whispered to me to grab the coat while Robin was playing and take it to the pawnshop. I grabbed the coat and flew out the door like a rocket, over to the pawn with it. When the game was over, Robin went berserk when he noticed it missing. "Where's my coat?" he roared, looking at me.

Eileen Begley, who worked at the mineral bar in the Corinthian, slips on the floor. Thankfully, Liam Begley was on hand to help her to her feet again.

Two happy couples, Neilly McCarron and Jean Moran with Sheena Anderson and Seamus Cusack, relaxing at the mineral bar in Borderland in 1964.

'Shrugging my shoulders, I pulled the pawn ticket from my pocket, and said, "Here it is. And don't worry, Robin, we'll get it out on Friday for you."

'That Friday, we got the coat out of the pawnshop and he was a relieved man. He gave us some stick but ended up laughing his head off about it with us after.

'Several weeks later, I was taking Jean to the pictures and Robin was going to a dance that same night. This time *he* had a problem: his suit was in the dry-cleaners and he had no money to lift it. He asked me for a loan of my suit for the night and I, of course, agreed. Next day, we met up as usual and I asked him for my suit back. Looking me straight in the eye, he pulled a pawn ticket out of his pocket and said, "Here it is. Sure don't worry, Neilly, I will lift it on Friday for you!"

'I never loaned him my suit again, and he never took that coat off his back again. He is probably looking down on me from above and laughing at me as I speak.'

The other thing Neilly remembers was the night Dickie McManus brought the house down in the Corinthian, singing that old Irish ballad *Boolavogue*. Neilly continues: 'That was a real show stopper that night. I was dancing with Jean and the floor was packed. Dickie was singing *Boolavogue* and nobody, but nobody, could sing it quite like him. The crowd on the dance floor stopped dancing. I'm not codding, you could have heard a pin drop. Everyone just stood still and listened to Dickie singing. He brought the place to a standstill, and even the bouncers came in from the front door to hear him. As he finished the song, everyone in the hall clapped, cheered and stamped their feet in appreciation of a class singer. The ovation he got that night was something I can still remember to this day. These are wee moments which you never seem to forget, moments that even time itself, can't erase from your mind.'

Robin Matchett.

The Woodchoppers' Dickie McManus is mobbed by fans at the Cameo in 1964.

Derry Dance-Hall Legends

When talking about the dance halls of that era, the names of Derry legends James MacCafferty, Johnny Quigley, Josie and Gay McIntyre, Stan Cauley, Willie Campbell, Willie Bradley, Mick 'The Voice' McWilliams, Harry Harkin, Eddie 'Every Voice' Kerr, George Hasson, and Dickie McManus always spring up.

After the war, James MacCafferty formed the Carlton Swingtette and was soon joined by Mick McWilliams. The Corinthian Ballroom owner, Jim Lecky, hired them as their resident band, and they proved so popular that this arrangement lasted for a solid eight years. The Lakewood Swingtette then took over the mantle as resident band and Mick McWilliams continued as their lead singer. In some ways, that provided continuity and they entertained the regular dance-goers in the Corinthian for many years after.

Mick McWilliams was widely regarded as the most talented singer of that era in Derry, and people flocked to the dances in the Corinthian and elsewhere when he was performing.

During the heady days of the Derry music scene, many top international stars appeared in St Columb's Hall and other local venues. And the yardstick by which many a concert-goer judged them was Mick McWilliams. Few, if any, were regarded as his equal. Jim 'Spud' McCready commented many years ago that some of the big stars were not at all pleased if they had to follow Mick McWilliams on stage.

A band of legends: Jim McDermott, Jimmy McIntyre, Barney Coyle, Josie McIntyre, Mick McWilliams and James MacCafferty in the Plaza Ballroom, Buncrana, in the early 1950s.

The very popular Lakewood Swingtette, featuring Mick McWilliams, who were resident for many years at the Corinthian Ballroom, Derry.

James MacCafferty with his Little Gaelic Singers in the late 1950s. Over the years, they impressed audiences worldwide at concerts and on television, including the one-and-only Elvis Presley.

Elvis Presley and the Little Gaelic Singers

Certainly, James MacCafferty and Mick McWilliams were involved in many a great night's entertainment in their home town, but even they could not have envisaged being present at arguably the most historical occasion in the history of Rock & Roll.

It happened like this …

On the night of Sunday 28 October 1956, James, Mick and the Little Gaelic Singers were appearing on the top television programme at that time in the USA, the *Ed Sullivan Show*. This was, and still is to this day, considered to be the greatest variety show in prime-time television history. It was the show which introduced the Beatles to the American nation.

This particular night, it was going out coast to coast in America and was being watched by over sixty million viewers. But what James and Mick didn't realise at the time was they were about to play a part in not only the most memorable occasion in the history of this show but arguably of Rock & Roll itself.

James, laughing loudly, admitted on the BBC Radio Foyle programme *Coyle and Co* that although over sixty million people were glued to their screens that night, probably not all of them had tuned in to see them, as appearing on the same show was an up-and-coming young American singer with great potential – Elvis Presley!

Elvis Presley singing Hound Dog *and wearing that emerald-green coat on the* Ed Sullivan Show *on Sunday 28 October 1956.*

Elvis Presley's scheduled appearance on the show had created serious controversy across the USA and was causing quite a stir among the older generation. Some newspapers voiced concerns about the suitability of airing such provocative and sensual movements on television ie Presley's pelvic gyrations. The dailies had run headline stories throughout the week about the pending appearance of Presley on the show and almost the entire population of teenage and adult America tuned in to see Elvis perform. The whole nation was divided in their opinion of the singer.

James MacCafferty went on to tell radio presenter Seán Coyle: 'We were standing at the side of the stage after coming off from doing our part on the show. Elvis came over and started to chat to us. He was fascinated with the Little Gaelic Singers, who were all dressed in Irish national costumes. When we told him we were from Ireland, Elvis said, "How nice. In that case, I will wear a green coat when I come back to do my second spot on the show." We were delighted with such a lovely gesture from this nice, friendly young man. When Elvis returned twenty minutes later to finish the show, he was, as promised, wearing an emerald-green coat.'

This performance, in which he sang *Hound Dog*, is regarded as Presley's most iconic TV appearance of all time, because this was the first occasion that a television camera crew had shown him on stage from the waist down. Even today, clips of the performance are still shown around the world when the origins of Rock & Roll are discussed. Among the other songs Elvis sang on that historic night was *Love Me Tender*, just days after it was released.

With the camera crew showing Elvis in full swing from head to toe, this, as predicted, caused uproar across America. Following the programme, an effigy of him was burned by crowds in Nashville and St Louis. The national press gave critical reviews of his style and gyrations on the night. The *Ed Sullivan Show* official website records the incident in its Rock & Roll archive with the following additional information:

Following an innocent act by an Irish children's choir, the Little Gaelic Singers, Elvis Presley took the stage. During one of his songs, the camera moved to a close-up of his face, and then, as if on cue, he smiled and curled his upper lip and the studio audience went wild.

That performance by Elvis was regarded as a defining moment in Rock & Roll, because at that time, Rock & Roll was being attacked from all quarters of the establishment; it was perceived by some as having a negative influence on the youth of America. However, the more the establishment condemned it, the more Elvis's support grew from millions of young people. As a result of Elvis appearing on the *Ed Sullivan Show*, the whole of America, and eventually the world, had to accept that Rock & Roll was here to stay.

The rest, as they say, is history.

Derry's finest, the James MacCafferty Singers, who evoke the fondest of memories in people throughout Ireland and further afield wherever Derry folk have spread.

Shortly after that show, Mick McWilliams was back on stage in the Corinthian Ballroom with the Lakewood Swingtette. And James MacCafferty was back rehearsing for future concerts with his multitalented team of singers.

James MacCafferty is regarded, and rightly so, as the man mainly responsible for nurturing the musical talent of the youth of Derry over many years. His contribution to the reputation that the city enjoys as the most musical in Ireland is immeasurable. James became ever present on the concert scene, performing often at Bishop Daly's renowned Sunday-night concerts in St Columb's Hall. These concerts became very popular and Derry people eagerly looked forward to them every week, as it was maybe the only outing a mother or grandmother got that week. Many internationally famed artists appeared there, with Jim Reeves perhaps being the biggest star to grace the famous old stage.

James also formed the famed MacCafferty Singers, which boasted the best of Derry's vocalists, and their line-up was a 'who's who' of local talent in the city. They were an absolute treat to listen to and watch. It was very evident that they really loved singing together, and the joy James MacCafferty and his singers gave to the people of Derry was immense.

The beauty of those concerts in St Columb's Hall was that they could be enjoyed by both young and old. I personally had my first experience of seeing a real star in the flesh at one of the shows at the tender age of fourteen. That star was Joe Brown, and he was appearing with his band, the Bruvvers. I remember all the seats were sold out, but the attendant ushered me and my mates along the side wall of the hall, where we just stood and watched this master on stage. We were mesmerised as Joe Brown thrilled the packed venue.

I met Pat MacCafferty, son of James, at John 'Jobby' Crossan's house and we reminisced about the concerts in St Columb's Hall. Pat also remembered being at the Joe Brown show that night and he readily confirmed that Joe was one of the best musicians he ever saw or heard. High praise indeed. A whole book could, and should, be written about James MacCafferty and his contribution to the musical tuition and entertainment of the people of Derry. The sheer joy he gave to people who had the privilege of seeing him with his singers will never be forgotten. The MacCafferty School of Music lives on today and is directed by James's daughter Úna Ó Somacháin.

Pat MacCafferty and his girlfriend Jean Rush enjoying a night out.

Rock & Roll and Jiving Around

In the mid-1950s, the world was rapidly changing. The Russians sent the Sputnik I spaceship to orbit the earth. Film idol James Dean became a cult figure for rebellious youth. And Derry was about to be shaken to the core as Rock & Roll got its local seal of approval in William Street on Tuesday 23 October 1956.

This happened when Bill Haley and his Comets rocked the City Cinema with their film *Rock Around The Clock*. This film drove Derry teenagers into a frenzy. Some just couldn't contain themselves; they jumped from their seats and started jiving in the aisle of the cinema. However, contrary to what most people believe, it was not the teenage boys but the teenage *girls* who actually started jiving in the aisles. The boys took their lead from the girls and started jiving when the film was over, and they carried on jiving right out into the middle of William Street. Buses to Creggan and Rosemount were halted as crowds gathered to watch the jivers. The

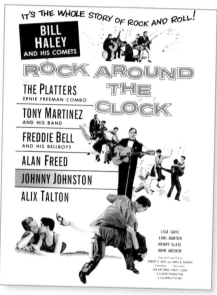

Tuesday 23 October 1956 – the night Rock & Roll arrived in Derry! Advert for the film Rock Around The Clock *in the City Cinema in William Street.*

CITY CINEMA

ALL WEEK :   Cont. from 2.05
Johnny Johnston, Lisa Gaye,
Bill Haley and his Comets in

Rock Around the Clock
2.55, 5.05, 7.20, 9.30

police moved them and the numerous onlookers on to Rossville Street, where, according to the *Derry Journal*, 'noisy scenes' took place. The jivers danced on to the Diamond and finally to Bishop Street where nervous police reinforcements arrived. But the crowds and jivers had had their fun by then and dispersed, exhausted but happy.

33

CROWDS DANCE IN STREETS:
WINDOWS BROKEN

ROCK 'N' ROLLERS CREATE NOISY SCENES

Police reinforcements were called out last night in Derry to deal with noisy scenes in the city centre when a crowd of juveniles "jived" through some of the principal thoroughfares following the showing of the rock 'n roll film, "Rock Around the Clock," in the City Cinema.

Crowds began to gather in William Street outside the cinema from about 10.30 p.m.; shortly before the screening was due to finish. When the cinema audience began to emerge several juveniles began to dance in the carriageway and the crowd gathered around to watch. Passing traffic was disrupted for about ten minutes and buses on the Rosemount and Creggan routes were hammered on the body panels by a section of the crowd.

The police got the crowd to move along and they then assembled in Rossville St., where similar noisy scenes took place. A section then moved to The Diamond and here again traffic was held up as dancing continued in the carriageway.

Several of the crowd clambered over the War Memorial and a wreath and its pedestal were flung to the ground by a youth.

The crowd then mobbed a nearby telephone kiosk where a constable was attempting to put through a call to Victoria Barracks for reinforcements and a pane of glass in the booth was broken, pieces of glass narrowly missing the constable's face.

Later it was found that four windows in the Apprentice Boys' Memorial Hall had been broken and that glass in the premises of Mr. A. Canning, flesher, Butcher Street, had also been broken.

A section of the crowd later formed again in Rossville Street where, cheered on by a large number of spectators, they jived on the street. They then visited Bogside, approximately one hour after the conclusion of the film show, where the final remnants of the gathering broke up.

A police spokesman, commenting on the scenes last night, said that the crowd was good tempered. It was just a few hooligans outside who decided that it was an occasion to break a few windows. Everything had been normal inside the cinema, he said, until a few minutes from the end when some of the spectators began to clap and stamp their feet.

Asked by a "Journal" reporter last night if there was a possibility of the run of the film being discontinued, Mr. W. Doherty, of the City Cinema, said that as far as the cinema management was concerned they were willing to co-operate with the local authorities in whatever action they wished to take.

He said that when the film was passed by the Corporation the cinema had been committed to a contract regarding its showing. It was really up to the authorities to take what action they considered necessary, he said.

"We are willing to co-operate fully with them in that," Mr. Doherty added.

Mr. Doherty said that the film had gone down quietly—"almost too quietly"—until within a few minutes of the conclusion of the last showing

Derry Journal report of 24 October 1956 on the disturbances in William Street after the film Rock Around The Clock *was shown the day before in the City Cinema.*

Liam Wray, a 1950s Teddy Boy, roars with laughter when he thinks back to that night. 'Although only a teenager, I remember standing in amazement as I watched Daniel 'Shava' Gillespie, Jock Henderson, Sonny Casey, Frankie Roddy, Terry McCloskey, 'Wang' McCann and Seamus McDevitt jiving in the middle of William Street. The crowds were clapping and cheering them on; the louder they cheered, the more adventurous the jivers got. Buses and cars were at a standstill. It was sheer bedlam, but great fun. It was the major talking point in Derry for weeks, and it now has its own special place in Derry folklore.'

Rock & Roll was here to stay, and although jiving may have been frowned upon by some dance-hall owners and promoters in the mid-1950s, it quickly became the youngsters' favourite. The Criterion Ballroom organisers, to their credit, soon realised that the jive was

The man who set William Street alight in October 1956, Daniel 'Shava' Gillespie and his wife Frances, jiving in a competition in the Stardust in 1990.

the dance of the future, and permitted jiving everywhere on the dance floor. It became so popular that other dancers stood around and watched as jivers gyrated and swirled throughout the venue.

Slowly, other hall owners realised too that they had no option but to follow suit. They accepted that the jive was the preferred dance of a growing number of the younger dance-goers. Of course, their decision was tempered by purely business reasons, as the youngsters were the paying customers of the future. Later, some of the dance-hall owners admitted that they thought it was just a passing phase that would burn itself out quickly. Soon, however, jiving couples were dancing in every corner of the dance floor and 'proper' dancers just had to waltz around them. The jive had arrived and was to change the dance-hall scene forever.

While the sight of hundreds of couples dancing the waltz in formation in the same direction was a lovely sight, and beautiful as it was, it had had its day. Although not totally 'extinct', it became a rare sight in the modern dance-hall scene which was now witnessing not only a different dance style but an altogether different dress style as well. It was without doubt a culture shock to the older dancers' system, as they now gave way to the arrival of the young, vibrant teenagers of the day.

And, boy, did they arrive with a bang!

Jackie Bonnar and Dickie McManus serenading the dancers in a traditional waltz in the Plaza, Buncrana, in the 1950s.

Now a regular feature on the traditional waltz, tango and quickstep-dominated dance-hall scene was the modern, all-action, pelvic-gyrating, jiving teenagers.

Enter the young men dressed in Teddy Boy suits and suede shoes, with shoelace-thin ties and sporting the new DA (duck's arse), Brylcreem-laced hairstyle. And leading from the front was the original Derry Teddy Boy, Terry McCloskey.

Not to be outdone, Lily Hegarty and her friends of the fairer sex came dressed in multicoloured can-can dresses, with bobby socks and matching hair bands. While jiving, every muscle was brought in to action as they danced the night away to the upbeat sound of *Rock Around The Clock* and *Johnny B Goode*, all trying new moves and trying to upstage each other.

What a difference in sound, from the tranquil and beautifully melodic *Mona Lisa* to the driving, fast-paced *Rock Around The Clock*.

What a difference in dance style, from the sedate but elegant waltzes of the late 1940s and early '50s, to the all-action, energy-sapping jive.

Although the contrast couldn't have been starker, there was no turning back now; the dance scene was irreversibly changed forever.

It was enough to make the purist think the world had gone mad!

The can-can girls dressed to thrill. Sheila Kelly, Maura Callan Peggy McLaughlin and Molly Kelly waiting for the bus to take them to the Diamond on their way to the Corinthian, 1961.

*The Corinthian crawl gang, Phil Cunningham, Ann Kelly, James McIntyre,
Maeve O'Connell and Mickey McCann in 1958.*

Seeking Work and Romance

Well-known Derry author Phil Cunningham readily admits work in Derry in the
1950s was scarce and any employment that could be got was poorly paid. Phil recalled his teenage years and how he and his mates had had a few skirmishes with the
Royal Navy men, both outside and inside the dance halls.

'It wasn't because you didn't like them, as you didn't know them personally, it was
simply at times just for the fun of it, and we were only about sixteen at the time. I
remember we played a trick on one of our mates once, Jimmy Lynch. We agreed we
would hide in a doorway, and if he went out and stopped a sailor and started a fight
with him, we would jump in and save him and 'rough up' the sailor. Jimmy did his
bit alright and tackled one of them. But we cleared off and left him to fight the boy
on his own. About fifteen minutes later, we went to find him and he came walking
up the street with a big black eye! That was the last time any of us started a fight
with a Navy men in the street.

'We were sixteen years old when we went to our first dance in the Criterion.
None of us could dance so we spent the whole night trying to force each other to go
and ask a girl out to dance. We ended our first dance, and none of us had gone onto
the floor the whole night.

'At that time, I was working as an apprentice barman in the Atlantic Bar in Foyle
Street and trying to learn the trade.'

Although working in the '50s was something to be thankful for, Phil was still not
contented. The bar owners didn't seem to trust the younger bar staff.

'I remember if I served a customer I had to give the money to the head barman
to ring in to the till, and then he would give me the change to give to the customer.
Imagine that happening today in a bar,' Phil added in disbelief.

It was while having a conversation with Danny Gallagher, a customer in the bar, who had just returned from Watford, England, that Phil learned that work was plentiful there. This started Phil thinking, so he quizzed Danny in detail about the place. By the end of the conversation, Phil was convinced that that is where he should be. 'Well, look, if you are serious, I can give you my return ticket, as I am not going back,' Danny told an excited Phil.

Phil went home and told his parents he was thinking of going to Watford to see if he could get a better job and make himself some money. His parents gave him their blessing on condition he went to Mass every Sunday. Phil relayed Danny Gallagher's story about Watford to his two mates Mickey Rush and Junior Havelin, and they decided they would go with him. So all three Derry boys set sail on the Heysham boat.

However, after working there for a year, the pull of his hometown was too much and Phil returned home. Soon, he started work as a helper on one of WG O'Doherty's lorries delivering crates of bottled stout to the local bars.

'I met up with all my old mates again,'

Phil Cunningham with Mickey Rush and Junior Havelin in Watford, 1954.

Bestselling author Phil Cunningham and Rosita Heaney on their honeymoon in Dublin in 1960.

Phil continued, 'who were now seasoned dancers and back to the Crit we all went. I eyed up this girl one night and went over to her and asked her for a dance. She just looked at me and I thought she was going to say no, but she didn't and we danced. We got chatting and she told me her name was Rosita Heaney. After the dance I was walking her home, thinking she lived in Creggan like me. When I got to Waterloo Place I turned to go up to Creggan. "Where are you going?" she asked. "I live in Pennyburn." At that time (1958), I thought Pennyburn was out in the country. Anyway, when I got to her house, I asked her did she want to go to the pictures on Monday night and she agreed. We went to the Midland in the Waterside and it was freezing. I remember she had the flu and for some reason I didn't see her again for six months. Again it was at the Crit and this time I made a beeline for her on the floor and we started going steady after that. We married in Pennyburn Church in 1960.'

Jitterbugging and Navy Men

In the pre-'spit-on-me, Dickie' days, the beehive hairstyles and can-can-dressed teen-age girls jiving the night away with teenage James Dean look-alikes, with their skin-tight trousers and winkle-picker shoes, were, I am told, a sight to behold.

Indeed, while talking to a group of ladies who were keen dancers at the time, they paint a rosy picture of life back then. They consistently reminded me that the young women of their era, who danced regularly in the local dance halls, were, by nature, shy, graceful, genteel creatures, who neither drank, smoked nor used bad language. They also were not slow in reminding me they never frequented bars. They preferred instead to stroll arm-in-arm along Carlisle Road, Strand Road or Shipquay Street, whispering and giggling together, with eyes cast shyly downwards when a male came into close proximity.

Puzzled, I asked how did the young men back then react to this shyness in the fairer sex. 'Ah, the same way as the men before them and the men after them did: they turned tail and headed for the nearest pub!'

I looked at them with raised eyebrows and a questioning gaze.

'Look, son, don't take our word for it, just ask any bouncer who was on the doors back then. They'll tell you the same thing. The Derry men needed to be 'well oiled' before they had the courage to make that first contact and ask you for a dance, never mind ask you for a date. But the sailors strolling around Derry, all heading to the local dance halls, they were a lovely sight,' they enthused.

And the American sailors were a joy to watch as they waltzed or jitterbugged around the Corinthian or Crit dance floors. They brought the American ballroom flair to Derry and they relished the candle-waxed dance floors as they just seemed to glide around the halls.

Ann Harkin, Vera Sheerin, Mary Clifford, Clare Bridge, Helen Kelly and Agnes Loughrey having a great time at the City Factory annual dance at the Embassy in 1965.

This young man is turning on the charm and sweet-talking his lady friend at a dance in the Guildhall in 1958.

On the bus on their way to a dance are the 'Lisahally Babes' Dolores Monaghan and Ann Starrett in 1963.

The ladies continued: 'Look at the many Derry girls who left these shores and followed their hearts, all the way to the different states of America, Canada and England to marry their sweethearts. Most are still in those countries and have reared families there. We see some of them occasionally when they come back to Derry on holiday.'

'How did the Derry men react to the sailors from various countries in the dance halls?' I asked.

'The local fellows were jealous of all the sailors who frequented the dance halls in the 1950s and early '60s. The sailors, especially the Americans, were lovely, romantic young men, with good manners, who treated ladies with respect. And, boy, could they dance! Not only were they gentlemen, they brightened up the dance halls with their slick uniforms and cultured American accents. To tell you the truth, the minute they opened their mouths, they melted your heart away. Just a pity I couldn't snare one for myself,' chuckles Margaret from Creggan with a wide smile.

The teenage girls of the '50s all agreed that after a long week working in the shirt factories they looked forward to the weekends.

One of the Maiden City's finest. Miss Ireland, Irene O'Kane, from Patrick Street, Derry, in the early 1960s.

40

Two couples enjoying a drink in Ken's Den on Carlisle Road before moving on to the Corinthian Ballroom in 1963.

'It's our memories of those days that keeps us smiling, isn't it, girls?' said Christine, looking for a nod of approval from the rest.

'Definitely. I can still visualise Dickie McManus singing *Boolavogue* on the stage of the Crit, Corinthian or the Guildhall. The sound of Johnny Quigley's band singing *Yakety Yak*, or Mick McWilliams singing *Blue Moon*. And the lovely sight of two hundred couples waltzing around the dance floor,' said Margaret.

When asked how they coped with the transition from can-can dresses to the miniskirt, there was an awkward silence. Margaret again answered first. 'It took a while, to be honest, but, my God, it did cut down on the material a girl needed for a skirt. Also, it cut the time a girl needed to get ready for a dance, and passing someone on the stairs was a lot easier.'

Christine chimed in. 'A Sunday night was great also; all the young ones from every part of Derry would congregate in Carlisle Road. And we would all parade up one side and down the other until about ten-thirty, and then it was a rush to get home to listen to the Top Twenty on Radio Luxemburg.'

Asking them if they can remember some of the songs from that time, Isobel enters the conversation and rattles them off in a flash. 'Songs like *Love Letters In The Sand*, *Blueberry Hill*, *Magic Moments*, *Story Of My Life* and *Love Me Tender*. To be honest with you, I still get butterflies when I think of those days. We can honestly say those were the best times of our lives, isn't that right, girls?'

Ann Sweeney and her pal Breege McLaughlin get their photograph taken at Derry Quay in August 1959 by Breege's boyfriend, American sailor Dave McConnell. In the background is Dave's ship, the USS Dealey.

Magic Moments at the Crit

On Thursday 20 August 1959, one of those young cultured American sailors was visiting Derry for the first time and, unknown to himself, was about to meet his partner for life that night.

He was on board the *USS Dealey* which sailed up the River Foyle and docked at the quay after a long trip from Newport, Rhode Island. On board was twenty-year-old Dave McConnell, a young sailor from Ohio. He remembers he was look-ing forward to the off-shore leave and the fact that it was a month-long leave in an English-speaking port made it all the better. 'I was excited as I walked down the gangway of my ship with my mates on this, our first night in Derry. Little did I know it would change the rest of my life forever.'

At the same time as Dave was making his way into the town centre, three young teenage girls, Breege McLaughlin, Ann Sweeney and Sadie Porter, were catching the 9.10pm bus from Springtown Camp on their way to a dance in the Criterion.

Dave takes up the story.

'The first night in town, we left our ship with much excitement; we walked to the Strand Road and strolled on towards Foyle Street. My first reaction to being on the streets of Derry was how happy and cheerful the people were, smiling faces everywhere and so friendly, and their brogue was just lovely. The first bar we saw was the Oregon Bar, and we decided to go in and taste their beer.

'To our surprise the beer was warm, as they had no ice in it. After a few more drinks, we left and walked on down Foyle Street, where we heard music coming from the upstairs of a building. We were curious about where the music was coming from and some people walking past told us it was a dance hall called the Crit. We decided to go in and see what it was like. We climbed the stairs and paid our admission money and stepped into the dance hall proper.

'The place was packed with people dancing all over the floor. We stood there for a while and just observed the dancers, who were jitterbugging like nobody's business. After a little while, we decided to dip our toe in the waters, so to speak. We had seen these two girls dancing on their own, so my mate and I went over to them and asked if we could please have this dance. And they said, "Sure, why not."

'During the dance, we exchanged pleasantries. I found out her name was Breege and I told her my name and a little about myself. We hit it off straightaway and we danced the whole night together after that. After the last dance, I asked if I could leave her home. She agreed.

'We chatted as we walked from the dance hall down the Strand Road and then turned left up the Rock Road. At the top of the Rock Road, Breege told me, "This is where your train stops." It was as far as I was allowed to go with her. She walked with her friends Ann Sweeney and Sadie Porter on towards their home on their own, but before she left me we agreed to meet the next day outside Littlewoods. It was only later that I found out she lived in Springtown Camp. And it was out of bounds for us!

'We met as planned the next day at Littlewoods corner and went for a walk around the town. The following night, we went to the cinema. During my month's stay in Derry, we went to several dances in the Crit and once we travelled to the Plaza in Buncrana and really enjoyed that.

'When my ship left Derry for London on Sunday 20 September 1959, it was with a heavy heart that I stood on deck and waved goodbye to Breege standing on Derry Quay. We agreed to write to each other and we did so twice a week for three long years.

'I had invited Breege over to visit me in America many times and eventually she agreed to come. So on Wednesday 30 May 1962, I finally saw her smiling face once more as she stepped off the plane. It had been three long years since we parted and I was determined to make sure we would never be parted again. Just over two months later, on 6 August 1962, we were married in Toronto, Ohio, USA. We have one son and we now live in Virginia Beach, Virginia.

'We always look forward to visiting Derry as often as we can, as it will always be home as far as Breege is concerned. While in Derry, we never fail to go and have a nostalgic look at the former Crit building in Foyle Street, where we first set eyes on each other all those years ago.'

Dave McConnell, who met his wife-to-be Breege McLaughlin in the Criterion Ballroom (the Crit) on his first night ashore in Derry in 1959.

Ireland's No 1 showband, the Johnny Quigley All Stars, playing at Borderland in 1960. Michael Quigley, Edmund Quigley, Johnny Quigley, Joe Quigley, Dennis Fisher, Bobby Forsyth, Roy Addinell, Thomas McMenamin and Jackie Flavelle.

Derry's All-Star Bands of the 1950s & 1960s

In the late 1950s, the Woodchoppers, under the leadership of Willie Bradley, were a big hit with dancers everywhere. They were regulars in all of the local dance halls and, like most other Derry showbands, travelled extensively to play in ballrooms across Ireland. Brass instruments were the main sound on stage at that time.

Willie recalls the showband days were hard, as you could be sitting in a van for six or seven hours, travelling to and from some of the remotest places in Ireland in all sorts of weather. Although difficult, those days were also very enjoyable, as the craic and banter in the van was mighty. Around the late 1950s, a fee of between £40 and £60 was the norm for a showband, depending on their popularity. They often got to share a stage with some world-famous stars when they appeared at the Corinthian Ballroom and other good venues.

The best-known Derry showband was, without doubt, the Johnny Quigley All Stars. They were Ireland's top showband at the turn of the '60s and drew massive crowds to their dances. Their name was apt, as they indeed were a band of star performers. Led by the famous Johnny Quigley, they added an American flavour to their repertoire when Michael (Johnny's brother) brought some new arrangements back from the USA. These exciting American hit songs added greatly to their programme which went down a treat with the dancers in all the ballrooms.

The Woodchoppers in the Plaza in the late 1950s. Note the basic PA equipment perched on chairs. Includes Willie Bradley, Jackie Bonnar and Dickie McManus.

The All Stars big band used thumping brass arrangements and could switch at ease from Rock & Roll and chart hits to waltzes, Latin-American and Dixieland. With no other showband playing such a range of material, they soon became a great attraction for dance promoters across Ireland. Their show was also enhanced by their quick dress changes, from ordinary band suits to jazzy yellow blazers and brown trousers as the music mood dictated.

Such was their fame and popularity throughout Ireland that they were booked by the management of the famous Ballymena ballroom, the Flamingo, to play on their gala opening night on Monday 12 December 1960. Even to this day when down south on weekend breaks or holidays, when you tell music lovers of a certain generation you are from Derry, they would still ask about Johnny Quigley and his All Stars.

It would be impossible when considering star performers from Derry not to mention the imperious Gay McIntyre and his band, who were known and revered the length and breadth of Ireland in the late 1950s, and '60s. It was easy to see why they enjoyed such fame, as Gay surrounded himself with top-class musicians such as trumpeter Roy Addinell, trombonist Johnny Anderson, drummer Tommy Mc-Menamin and his own brother, Joe.

The Gay McIntyre Band with Gerry Anderson, Jim 'Fontaine' McGonagle, George Hasson, Gay McIntyre, Liam Griffin and Colum Arbuckle.

Gay is regarded by many of his fellow musicians as the most talented musician in Derry. George Hasson, who played on numerous records cut at the famed Eamonn Andrews studio in Dublin, opined, 'Gay McIntyre is not only the best in Derry, but was, and still is, one of the best alto sax players in Europe. I firmly believe you could drop Gay off in any country in the world and he could play with the top musicians or bands of that country. He could slot into any band, anywhere, no matter how high the calibre or exalted the company; he is a class apart. Simple as that.'

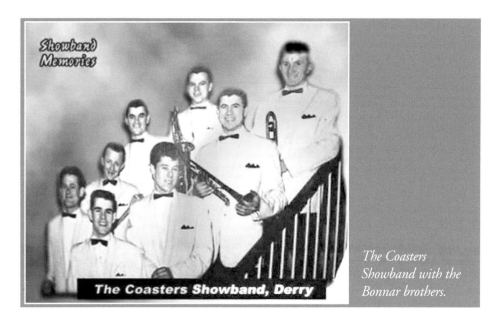

The Coasters Showband with the Bonnar brothers.

Top Ten Hits of the 1950s

In those days, audiences would have danced mainly to Rock & Roll music which was heavily influenced by American bands and singers. Their songs were played on a daily basis by the 'stations of the stars' – Radio Luxemburg and Radio Caroline. It is interesting to note that some of those tunes are just as popular today and still get plenty of coverage on many popular radio stations.

Let's take a wee dander down memory lane and have a look at the music that set the dance halls of the mid- and late 1950s alight.

The following were listed online as the top ten songs of the '50s. The list was based not only on the songs' record sales but on their lasting popularity and influence and impact on the evolution of Rock & Roll down the decades:

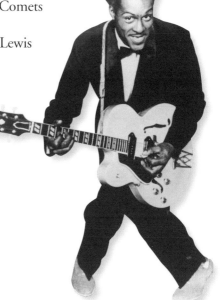

1 *Johnny B Goode* – Chuck Berry
2 *Rock Around The Clock* – Bill Haley & His Comets
3 *Jailhouse Rock* – Elvis Presley
4 *Whole Lot Of Shakin' Going On* – Jerry Lee Lewis
5 *Shake, Rattle And Roll* – Joe Turner
6 *Tutti Fruitti* – Little Richard
7 *Hound Dog* – Elvis Presley
8 *Long Tall Sally* – Little Richard
9 *That'll Be The Day* – Buddy Holly
10 *Blue Suede Shoes* – Carl Perkins

However, the top three bestselling records of the 1950s, based solely on sales in Britain and Ireland, were:

1 *Rock Around The Clock* – sold 1,390,000
2 *Diana* – sold 1,240,000
3 *Mary's Boy Child* – sold 1,170,000

Overleaf: Willie Bradley, band leader with the famed Woodchoppers, waves from the crowd to the photographer at the Embassy Ballroom in the early 1960s. Included are Kathy Durnin, Andy McCartney, John Coyle, Margaret Coyle, Johnny Patterson, Liam Dalton, Billy Norris, Jim McCallion, Kevin McKeever, Willie Deery (solicitor), Donal Ramsey, Billy McGrenara, Paddy McQuilkin, Agnes Hume, Harry Harkin and Josie McIntyre.

The Ray Gallagher Orchestra in the Corinthian in 1958. George Hasson, D Doherty, Johnny Stewart, Ray Gallagher, John Deehan, G Doherty and S Neeley.

Stealing the Limelight

It would be very difficult to name here the line-ups of all the Derry showbands who entertained audiences everywhere, not least because they kept changing personnel almost weekly. But here are just a few: the Magnificent Seven, known as the Mags, with the likes of Johnny Patterson; Imperial All Stars, with Don Carlin at the helm; Jimmy 'China Doll' Liddy, who played with showbands, country & western and even skiffle groups; the Jokers Showband, with the McMenamin brothers and Seamus McConnell.

There was always great rivalry between the Derry showbands as each sought to outdo the other and grab the limelight. This led to some spectacular stunts on stage which would not only surprise the crowd on the night but would keep them talking about it long after the dance was over.

One such fun stunt, which is still remembered by the Corinthian dancers, was carried out not by a showband star but by one of the regular dancers. *Tom Dooley* was a smash-hit record at the time. The song was about a man who was about to be hanged for murder. Word spread among regular Corinthian dance-goers that the hanging scene of *Tom Dooley* was going to be re-enacted on stage so the crowds flocked to this particular dance to see this stunt take place.

Tony O'Donnell, affectionately known as Tod, was a regular at the Corinthian. A great character, Tod was always up for a laugh so he readily agreed to do the part of Tom Dooley. The hanging scene was carried out on stage to roars of laughter and applause by the dancers. From then on, the names of Tod O'Donnell and Tom Dooley were inextricably linked by the Corinthian faithful. People of that era, to this day, still fondly remember that night.

Billy Tyson with the Esquires Showband looking through their programme for the night at the Corinthian in 1961.

If dance-goers thought that stunt was a one-off and couldn't be beat they were wide of the mark, as Billy Tyson proved!

Billy was lead singer with the Esquires Showband. Everyone who danced in the Corinthian Ballroom will remember the night Billy caused a sensation by dressing up in a skeleton suit. The said suit was painted in luminous paint, which showed the bones of the skeleton clearly. When Billy came on stage, it was arranged the lights would go out in the hall and the spotlight would shine on Billy. It worked to great effect and had the packed crowd in stitches. The stunt was talked about for ages afterwards and is still talked about to this very day. Billy enthused: 'We were playing in the Ierne Ballroom in Dublin about a month later, and people came up and asked me if I had the skeleton suit with me. It never ceased to amaze me how word travelled so fast around the halls of Ireland in those days.'

Peter Rogers, James Lecky (manager), Paddy 'Barman' Duffy, Nuala Lecky (daughter of the manager) and Patsy Begley at the entrance to the Corinthian in 1960.

Joe McCallion, Don Carlin, Patsy 'Yachts' McDermott and Harry Hamill during a dance in the Corinthian in 1959.

Billy also remembers the harder times. He recalls travelling one day with the band to a gig in Cork in a van which also carried all the instruments and sound equipment. The year was 1960 and for this gruelling round trip of fourteen hours, plus three hours on stage, he received the princely sum of £3.10s. He also recalls playing in Killarney one night and as they were on stage the snow fell from the sky. 'It fell so heavily that by the time the dance was over, it was so deep there was no chance of us being able to drive back to Derry. We had to stay in the hall and we slept in the dressing room with coats over us. That was a long night, I can tell you.

Joe McCallion, Mike McAllister, Gerry Doherty and Joe Ward celebrating before going to the Corinthian, 1962.

And to put the tin hat on it, the promoter cleared off without giving us our fee. He just disappeared into thin air. All we could do was to eat everything in his wee shop in the hall. That sort of thing didn't happen too often, to tell you the truth, but I think every band suffered one of those nights at the hands of a rogue promoter.

'Another awkward night I can remember was the night I was taken off the stage in the Corinthian by Paddy Kenny who was head of the musicians' union in Derry. The place was packed to the rafters and after singing the last song of a set, he beckoned Johnny McCollum and me down from the stage. He then quietly but firmly informed us, in his own inimitable way, that we were both behind in our union dues. Johnny was one shilling and sixpence and I was one shilling behind. We had to fork it out there and then before he would allow us to go on stage again. I will never forget that for as long as I live,' laughed Billy.

Billy later left the Esquires and joined top Sligo band the Clefonaires with whom he stayed for two happy years. I asked Billy if he'd do it all over again, and if so, would he do things differently.

'Yes, without doubt I would do it all again, because I saw places I would never have had the opportunity of seeing without being in a showband. To answer your question on what I would do differently, I would have to say I would seek a more professional management set-up to guide and promote the bands better.'

Mary Clifford chatting with a secret admirer in the balcony of the Corinthian in 1964.

These girls are making sure their cigarette packets and matches are not too far away!

Adverts from the Derry Journal. *Above, December 1955 and below, August 1968.*

Keeping On Your Toes

The travelling a showband had to undertake didn't bother the wife of one of Derry's best-known musicians.

Ann Wilkinson remembers the night she met trumpeter George Hasson in the National Ballroom in Dublin. 'The National was always packed to the rafters every Monday night. It was the in-place to be, because all the showband stars were normally there, as it was their night off. I was just going to hear the band, really, and had no notion of going with a fellow. But when I met George he soon changed my mind. He was quiet, well mannered and thoughtful, but it was his lovely brogue that first attracted me,' she laughs.

Ann went on to tell me she loved music, so dating a showband member was fine by her. She knew they travelled a lot, but if the band was playing nearby she would go and hear them. 'And anyway, it would have been the same as your husband being on night shift. No difference, really,' she added.

George, trumpeter with the Emperors, Woodchoppers and the Gay McIntyre showbands, was himself also only there to hear the band. He recalls: 'The National Ballroom on a Monday night was where the showband musicians would have gone to listen to the band and to relax. Whatever band was playing on a Monday night knew they would have to be on their toes, as a lot of musicians from a lot of different showbands would be in the hall. Also, it was a night when a musician who may not have been working could get a job with a showband, as musicians came and went often. Anyway, I wasn't looking for a job, as I was already playing with the Emperors, but I got myself a wife!'

Showband man George Hasson and Ann Wilkinson on honeymoon.

Carefree Years

Noel McBride, a well-known Derry celebrity and comedian, was a child of the 1950s. Speaking to him, it was evident he absolutely loved his carefree teenage dancing years. Noel admits he wasn't a frequent visitor to Borderland, as he preferred the Corinthian or the Crit.

'I had four mates and we went everywhere together. Actually, two of them, Mickey Cassidy and Em Dillon, were great singers and sang in Derry showbands. The other two were Jackie Higgins and Junior McLaughlin. As well as the Corinthian, we would be regulars in Battisti's café in Ferryquay Street. We would sit in the stalls and have a mineral and play the jukebox. Our favourite song then was *Only Make Believe* by Conway Twitty. It cost a threepenny bit to play a record, but we used to put a shilling in and play it four times.

'We also loved the Lakewood Swingtette with Mick McWilliams. Boy, what a singer, a massive talent. Relaxing at home at times, I just close my eyes and let my mind slip back to the Corinthian days and Mick singing *Begin The Beguine*. They played in the

— BUNCRANA INDUSTRIAL FUND —
presents
THE LAKEWOOD SWINGTETTE
with Mike McWilliams — The Voice
IN CORINTHIAN BALLROOM, DERRY
ON FRIDAY, 6th MARCH, 1959
DANCING 9—2 — ADMISSION 3 6
Buses leave Buncrana at 9 o'clock.
RETURN FARE — (including dance) — 8/-

Corinthian every Monday, Wednesday and Saturday night as the resident band and we were regulars at most of their dances. The memories just flood back when the very names of the Corinthian or Mick McWilliams are mentioned.

'I remember the night I first set my eyes on my wife Eleanor; it was, of course, at the Corinthian. I swear to God, I attempted to dance her about three times, but someone always beat me to it. So I thought to myself, I need to stand beside her and be the first to ask her for the next dance. So there I was, standing close by, waiting for the band to strike up the music, which would be my cue to approach Eleanor for the dance. And what do you think happened? They announced the next dance was

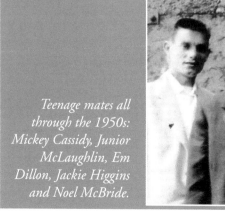

Teenage mates all through the 1950s: Mickey Cassidy, Junior McLaughlin, Em Dillon, Jackie Higgins and Noel McBride.

a Ladies' Choice! Now, back then, it was under the pain of mortal sin if you didn't return the dance to the last man who danced you.

'However, the next dance after that, I made sure it was my turn and I eventually got to dance her. We seemed to click straightaway, so I asked her to go for a mineral with me. Asking a girl to go for a mineral was the same as asking to leave her home then; same thing, really. Eleanor agreed, so off we went upstairs to the mineral bar in the Corinthian. After we had the minerals, we had another few dances and I walked her home that night. From then on, my four trusted friends took a back seat as Eleanor and I went everywhere together.

'It's a different ball game when you start to go steady, as opposed to running about with your mates. For instance, every Sunday, me and my mates would nor-mally stroll down the quay to look at the naval ships berthed there. The quay back then would have had more people walking up and down it than Shipquay Street has today. When I started going steady with El-eanor, I swapped walking down the quay with my mates to walking out a wee quiet country road with Elea-nor. And taking her to the pictures resulted in me getting slagged by my mates, instead of me slagging some other boy walking into the pictures with his girl. We got engaged on 10 December 1960 and we were mar-ried in the Waterside Church on 23 February 1963.

'When Eleanor and me are hav-ing a quiet night in, sitting at home chatting together, we at times remi-nisce and let our minds slip back to the days of the Corinthian and the fun-filled nights we enjoyed at the dances there. We inevitably end up laughing our heads off when we recall the antics of some of the characters of the time. And to be honest, when we look back on our courting days, we feel sorry for today's young people, because we had so much to do then, and they seem to have so little now.'

Well-known Derry comedian Noel McBride with his girlfriend, Eleanor O'Donnell, at the old football pitch at Irish Street, now Knockwellan Park.

The Imperial All Stars, featuring Don Carlin as lead singer.

Southern Showbands Come North

Just as the Derry ballrooms had it all to themselves until Borderland and the rest of the other Irish ballrooms came on the scene, the same applied to the local show-bands. The Derry bands had a great name throughout Ireland. It was a common sight to see upwards of twenty-five of them cross the bridge at weekends on their way to every part of the country to strut their stuff, with few if any southern showbands coming north. If there was one criticism of Derry musicians it was that they changed bands too often.

Willie Bradley, band leader of the Woodchoppers, commented, 'Every time you got a new photograph of the band taken, it was almost inevitable someone would leave the following week! That was a standing joke among musicians when a new photograph was arranged to be taken.'

The winter of 1959 saw the beginning of the end of the domination by Derry showbands in the dance halls and ballrooms in Ireland. And to make matters worse, it was about to happen in their own back yard. The news was carried in all the local newspapers. It read:

The Sensation of the Nation. The Royal Showband from Waterford are making their first visit to the North and will be playing in the Pallidrome in Strabane.

Was it just coincidence that Strabane was the place their manager TJ Byrne chose to play their first gig in the North? Or was it the case they were going into the lion's den, the home of the Clipper Carlton, who'd started the showband phenomenon, to prove a point? Maybe they thought if they go down well there, then they have made it.

On Monday night 23 November 1959, Strabane was buzzing with excitement as hundreds of people made their way to the Pallidrome ballroom. The dancers were anxious to see for themselves why so much fuss was made of this showband from Waterford. Was it all hype they were reading about this supposedly sensational showband? Well, now they could find out for themselves.

The Royal Showband from Waterford with Brendan Bowyer as the front man were the first southern showband to come north of the border when they played the Pallidrome, Strabane, in November 1959.

The most popular band in the South comes
North for the first time————THE

ROYAL SHOW BAND
(Waterford)

MAGIC BEAT .... MUSIC in the NEW STYLE

In the PALLIDROME, STRABANE
NEXT MONDAY NIGHT (Nov. 23rd)

Dancing 9-2   ADM. 5/-   Light snacks available in ballroom at moderate charges
This band cannot appear in these parts for at least two months
due to pressure of bookings.

They were not disappointed, as the energetic Brendan Bowyer and the Royal Showband brought the house down with a scintillating performance. The Derry contingent who had travelled to Strabane sang the band's praises in their workplaces during the following days. The Royal Showband made such an impression it was inevitable that their appearance in Derry (the hotbed of the showband scene) was imminent. A mere nine weeks later, they played in the splendour of Derry's Guildhall on Tuesday 19 January 1960.

The band's reputation preceded them, as it was the first time the Guildhall charged five shillings admission for any band. Despite the hike from the normal three shillings, the place was packed to the rafters and, as in Strabane, Bowyer and the Royal didn't disappoint. They proved a massive hit with the Derry dancers whom they not only sent home sweating but eagerly awaiting their return. This success was the prelude to a stampede of southern-based bands to the northern ballrooms and dance halls. The Capitol, the Miami, the Drifters and the Cadets all followed. With these showbands proving so popular with dancers, many other new showbands quickly appeared on the scene.

John Dunne and friends at the Plaza in 1966.

The Magnificent Seven Showband from Derry, named after the famous Western (even though they always had eight in the band). Included are the incomparable trio of Jimmy 'China Doll' Liddy, Johnny Patterson and Pat McCrossan.

The Emperors Showband with Charlie Dillon, George Hasson, Johnny Anderson, Eddie 'Every Voice' Kerr, George Sweeney, Jackie Boyd and Dessie Dillon providing the music for the dancers at the Embassy in 1964.

By now, the showband craze was sweeping Ireland and ballrooms began to spring up throughout the country. In almost every village, and in some very remote parts of rural Ireland, buildings of all types and sizes were hastily built and duly opened as ballrooms. Businessmen and some clergy became ballroom promoters overnight and for years after cashed in on the showband phenomenon. Some of the rural ballrooms were of such a primitive nature and were built with such haste that they didn't even have proper changing rooms. This necessitated the musicians having to change clothes in their vans, even on the coldest of nights.

With the emergence of the high-profile southern bands, who were managed by people who wielded great influence in the entertainment scene, the prognosis for the future of the Derry showbands looked bleak. Unfortunately, this proved to be the case, as the Derry bands were now falling behind in the pecking order of dance-hall promoters. They were now finding it increasingly difficult to get enough bookings to sustain a showband-size band. Some broke up into smaller groups and played the bar circuit locally, making a living without the long hours on the road. So for some local musicians, it actually worked out to their advantage.

On the question of how did the southern showbands push the Derry showbands off centre stage, Billy Tyson was forthright. 'They had better management than we had, so they were naturally better promoted than we ever were. No other reason. Simple as that. Because the Derry bands were highly regarded for their musical expertise everywhere.'

THE FLAMINGO BALLROOM, BALLYMENA

The Flamingo Ballroom in Ballymena, one of the better ballrooms that opened in the 1960s.

The Dixie Showband from Cork.

The original Miami Showband line-up with front man Dickie Rock.

George Hasson had a slightly different take on the reason. 'The southern show-bands without doubt had better sound equipment and were better managed. They received favourable publicity, and more of it, from southern newspapers. But they were definitely not better musicians, as there was no better showband, musically, in Ireland than the Johnny Quigley All Stars. However, to be fair to them, they were probably better showmen. And that, in my opinion, caught the imagination of the young dancers, and thus they became more popular.'

Jimmy Higgins, author of the excellent *Are Ye The Band?*, tends to agree with George's viewpoint. He had this to say: 'In general, northern bands were musically superior to their counterparts in the south.' However, he goes on to suggest the reason for this superiority was because of the availability of American Forces Network (AFN) radio and the influence of the American forces stationed in Derry. Jimmy maintains, 'This would have given Derry musicians access to big-band jazz music.' He also mentions that Derry children had the luxury of music tuition in schools, although this did not apply to all schools. He concludes by saying, 'The musicians also had the benefit of lots of time to practise because of the lack of employment in Derry.'

The late and much-missed Don Carlin summed it up perfectly when he said, in his own inimitable way, 'The Derry showbands had it great for years. We enjoyed a great reputation throughout Ireland and we played in every ballroom, hotel and dance hall in the country. Then the southern showbands came and knocked us off our perch, it's as simple as that, and fair play to them. They had the best of gear and were professionally managed by people who had great influence and great contacts, not only on the entertainment circuit but in the press as well.'

Danny McNally was a teenager in the 1950s. He, too, was sorry to witness the slow demise of the Derry showbands, as he thought they were brilliant. 'They provided local dancers like myself and my wife Frances with many happy memories.' However, he admits that the southern bands were colourful, energetic and gave their all on stage. 'Also, you couldn't read a newspaper without a southern showband's photograph being in it, coupled with a big write-up beside it.'

Danny remembers the local bands with great fondness. 'After all, it was the Woodchoppers who were playing when I had my first dance with Frances. However, I didn't meet her at a dance; I actually followed her onto a bus so I could get the opportunity to talk to her.' Danny continues as Frances looks on with a smile, 'Frances worked in Wilkinson's shirt factory on the Strand Road and I was working nearby as an apprentice electrician with the old UTA

A happy Ulster Transport Authority apprentice electrician Danny McNally keeps a tight hold of girlfriend Frances Doherty at a dinner dance in the old City Hotel in 1962.

(Ulster Transport Authority). I noticed she caught the same bus every night, so I decided I would do the same; it was the only way I could think of striking up a conversation with her. I was a shy lad, so for ages all I could do was say hello. Then, one night I somehow summoned up the courage to start a conversation with her. It was just small talk for a few days, but at least the ice was broken. Then, out of the blue, I found myself asking her would she go with me to the UTA dinner dance in the old City Hotel. She just looked at me and for a fleeting second my heart stopped, as I thought she was going to refuse, but thankfully she said yes.

'We had a great night and other dates followed. Soon we were dancing everywhere: Borderland, the Corinthian and the Guildhall. Those were brilliant times, innocent, carefree days, not a care in the world. Days when it seemed the sun shone every day, days neither of us will ever forget. Because those times were the start of a lifelong romance which is as strong today as it was way back then. And that was almost fifty years ago.'

Rest period for Bridget Gilmore, Frankie 'Spud' Murphy and Sarah Gilmore at the Embassy in 1971.

Daniel 'Shava' Gillespie with his bride Frances Kelly on their wedding day.

Above: Jimmy 'Friday' O'Kane and sister Maura taking part in the final of the Northern Ireland Jiving Championship in the Stardust at the Borderland reunion dance in 1990 in which they came third.

Below: A man who loved the 1950s look was Paddy Parson from Derry, seen here in his Teddy Boy gear in 1973.

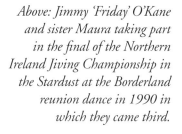

Tony Quigley waltzing around the Borderland floor with old friend Bernie Harkin in 1965.

The last ballroom manager in Derry, Raymond Rogan, with his wife Margaret. Raymond retired from managing the Stardust in 2004.

The Globetrotting Chippie

Another dancing-mad teenager of the '50s was William Street-born and reared Tony Quigley. Tony recalls he couldn't wait to leave school to start work and start dancing. Tony, a much-travelled Derryman who holds Irish, Canadian and Australian passports, takes up his story. 'Everyone can remember the day they started work for the very first time. The same can be said for that very first dance you went to and the very first girl you dated. Although small things, nevertheless they were momentous occasions in a young person's life and that is why they are easily recalled to memory. We may laugh at these memories now, but back then, your first job, first dance and first date were no small matters.

'I left the Christian Brothers School when I was fifteen years old and started work as an apprentice joiner with Frank O'Connor Builders in 1959. My first week's pay was one pound. It was exciting times for a young boy, and youthful exuberance was there in abundance. I can remember walking into the Criterion Ballroom for the first time, aged fifteen; I went with Paddy Hickey. The band playing that night was the Willie Campbell Showband. I can remember the very tune they were playing as I took my first tentative steps into the world of dancing. It was an oldie called *Alexander's Ragtime Band*. I knew it was an old tune, but Joe Henderson, who was dressed in a Teddy Boy suit, was jiving at a hundred miles an hour to it. I will never forget that feeling or the excitement I felt at that, my very first dance. Later, with my mates, we travelled to every dance hall within a twenty-mile radius of Derry. With thirty bob you could buy half a dozen stout, ten Park Drive or Woodbine, pay for the bus and still have the entrance fee to Borderland.'

Two happy young men with not a care in the world – Tony Quigley and Harry Hamill, seen here enjoying the craic at a dance in Borderland in 1965.

Even though he was just a teenager back in the late '50s, Tony said he knew the lifestyle he wanted, so he set himself goals. 'At that stage I made up my mind on several things regarding my life. I remember telling my mates that I wouldn't get married until I was over thirty, as I wanted to travel and see a bit of the world. Another thing I wanted to do was to go back to school and obtain some qualifications in my chosen profession as a vocational trades teacher.

For some, twenty-one years is a mighty long time, but not for these two childhood pals as they arrange to meet up again in 1986. This time their rendezvous was in Canada, 4,000 miles away from Derry. Tony and Harry may be looking slightly older, but I guess are a whole lot wiser.

'In the late 1960s, after working in England and Guernsey, I decided to emigrate to Canada and I told George Hutton, a fellow carpenter, of my plans and he decided to come with me. We were interviewed by the immigration staff and without further discussion, we bought our tickets. We arrived in Canada soon after and started work two days later. George came home about six months later, but I decided to stay on and stick it out. That was the start of my journey around the globe. So with one of my objectives now achieved, I put in motion my plans to obtain further education. To this end, I attended Queen's University, Canada, and was delighted to obtain a degree in technical studies with a teaching certificate.'

Another twenty-one years have passed when the boys from William Street and Waterloo Street meet up again at Niagara Falls in 2007. Their next meeting is planned for 2028 at the Crit in Foyle Street. All welcome.

Tony certainly has seen a bit of the world as he has travelled to over thirty differ-ent countries and was domiciled in Australia for many years. 'Thankfully, I can now look back with some degree of satisfaction, as I have achieved my objectives. I am proud to say that no matter where I travelled to, or how long I stayed away, Derry never left my mind. To be honest, if I went to a dance in Canada it would make me think back to my days at the Corinthian, Cameo or Borderland. And every St Patrick's Day there was a lump in my throat as I let my mind slip back to when I was a child growing up in William Street and attending the cathedral and singing 'Hail, glorious St Patrick, dear saint of our isle'.

'It was the same whenever I heard *Forty Shades Of Green* on the radio. I would think of home and all sorts of memories would come flooding back. A smile would come to my face when I thought of me and Harry Hamill meeting Paddy Henry, 'Boodgim' Doherty, 'Spud' Murphy and 'Friday' Kane on the Strand Road. Honest to God, we just couldn't pass each other without sparks flying. Those teenage years, all my old friends, all the old haunts like the Corinthian, the Crit, Borderland, the Embassy and the Cameo, were, and still are, a part of me. And no matter where you travel to, you never really forget home.'

Joe McCallion joined Tony and myself at our table in the Grianán Hotel restau-rant and both continued to reminisce about the showband years. Joe talked of the time he and his friends were barred from the Corinthian for a couple of dances be-cause they had a slight disagreement with some sailors which he admitted was prob-ably just pure jealousy on their part. He explained: 'When they were dancing with all the local girls, all you could hear was: "I'm from Texas," or "I'm from Arizona," or "I'm from Ohio," in swanky American accents. They were from far-off romantic places and they all seemed to be tanned, swarthy and good-looking, and they were slick movers on the dance floor to boot.

Opposite: Downing a few in O'Brien's Bar at McKeown's Lane before going to the Corinthian are Abbie McGuinness, PJ O'Neill, Mike McAllister, John McCafferty, Joe McCallion and Barry Mallett.

Right: Margaret Devine, Leo Quinn, John Curran and Tony Quigley meet up at the Cameo in 1965.

'I suppose we saw ourselves as pale faced, and our lingo was the basic Derry slang everybody spoke. And we could only say to the girls we were from Fox's Corner or William Street or Rossville Street. It's funny, really, when you think of it now, how immature we were. Because when you are away today, in England, America or Canada, you are very proud to tell people you are from Derry. Sure we had some great characters and everything we ever needed in Rossville Street we had.'

Joe continued with the following verses:

Pawnshops, boozers and some of life's losers,
Turf men, cattlemen, tinkers, hawkers and sailors,
Street-corner choirs in harmony singing,
Herring barrels smelling, ice-cream vendors yelling,
Women in pinnies, the day's gossip telling.

Toss pits, card schools, street marching bands,
Mince meat for stews bought in Kitty the Shans.
Factory girls walking with Yanks hand-in-hand,
Some of them now exiled in far-off distant lands.
Pride of our city, you worked as hard as any man.

Dot O'Donnell's bookies, Joe Cavanagh's poultry shop,
Ducks' eggs, country butter, Madden's soda pop.
A hosepipe fixed to the backyard tap, the only shower we got,
Hair oil, liquid paraffin, bay rum and Brylcreem, we used a lot.
Girls in can-can dresses learning to do the Corinthian hop.

Market day was such a sight, with all sorts of cows and sheep,
The banter and craic was great, deciding what was cheap.
On Saturday morning, the turf men sold their bags of peat,
Jockey Pepper and Big Buff, I'm sure, in Heaven have a seat.
Saints were few but devils none, in dear old Rossville Street.

Barry 'Bassy' Mallett, Mary Tierney, Jim McCallion, Michael Doherty, Danny McCallion and Joe McCallion in the lounge of the Matador Bar, Muff, before heading to Borderland in 1961.

Tony and Joe went on to tell of the night they missed their lift home from the Plaza in Buncrana and were arrested by the Gardaí. Tony continued: 'We were drinking, and to be honest, we were well tanked and were late leaving the dance. When we eventually came out, our bus was gone. Patsy Allen, a Derry girl, also missed the bus that night, so the three of us began walking home. Up the street we saw this bicycle outside a house, so we decided to 'borrow' it. I rode the bicycle, Joe was sitting on the handlebars and Patsy was on the wee rear carrier grid. We flew down the street in Buncrana and turned the corner heading for Derry. Suddenly, this big garda steps out to the middle of the street and stops us – and promptly arrests all three of us! They let Patsy go, but we were held in the cells overnight and had to wait until our parents came down the next day and bail us out. The owner of the bicycle, a garda, saw the funny side of it and refused to press charges. We got off with a warning.'

Joe, looking at a photograph of them as young men in the late 1950s, said, 'We never had much back then but we always took pride in how we dressed. Look at the seven of us in that photograph, all suited and booted, with shirt and tie! Getting fitted out in a new suit meant going up the town and into the likes of Burton's tailor shop or the Weaver to Wearer shop where you got measured, left a deposit and agreed to pay a weekly amount until the suit was paid for in full. It was the only way most people could afford a new suit then. When getting this type of credit, it was the norm to sign your name over a stamp with the queen's head on it, which seemed to constitute a legally binding contract between you and the tailor shops.'

Smartly dressed doormen lined up and ready for a busy night.

Bouncers and Matchmakers

Just as there were well-known bands, musicians and singers who graced the ball-rooms, the same can be applied to the doormen, or as they were commonly known, the bouncers.

These were the dickie-bowed men entrusted to 'keep the peace' at our dance halls. Their duty was to make entry to the ballrooms hassle free and to refuse access to any known troublemakers, or anyone who had consumed too much alcohol. Another part of their duty was to break up any fights that might erupt during a dance, and to evict the culprits as 'gently' and swiftly as possible. It is fair to say fights broke out from time to time, because if truth be told, there were a few self-proclaimed hard men attending the dances. These were mostly of the immature type whose antics were not designed to inflict major injury to anyone. Their actions were merely designed to try and impress the womenfolk and also to seek a reputation as a hard man. They seldom succeeded in their quest.

The bouncers were aware of such attention seekers and had little or no difficulty in dealing with them. Most of the doormen could spot a potential trouble-maker a mile away. They also had the knack of separating them from any young men who maybe were of a shy nature and needed a drink to enable them to ask a girl to dance, not to gain false courage for confrontation One such shy man admitted to me he needed to be 'well tanked' before entering a dance hall. He said the bouncers would just say, 'Look, son, take a wee walk, come back in fifteen minutes and we will let you in.'

Doing the door of Borderland on a quiet night are Gerald 'Stout' Ferguson, John Ferguson and Gerry Taggart in September 1970.

When the topic of bouncers cropped up, three men in particular would be mentioned in various conversations. They were Patrick 'Barman' Duffy, Gerald 'Stout' Ferguson and Danny Ogle. Although they were from different generations, they worked together at times.

Joe McCallion was among the many who considered that Barman Duffy was a legend of the ballrooms and a gentleman. Joe remarked: 'He was a class apart; he had the knack of just throwing you a glance which said "calm it". No doubt about it, he was the daddy of them all. Everyone, young and old, even the most wayward of young men, respected him; he carried that aura which very few people possess.'

It was obvious from people's memories of Barman Duffy that he was indeed a class apart. A great book has already been written about him and, suffice to say, he was regarded by everyone with fond respect.

'Dancers, showbands and bouncers, we all needed each other, simply because you couldn't have a dance without one of us.' These words were spoken by a man who should know – Stout Ferguson.

One of Derry's best-known bouncers, Stout, reminiscing about his days as a dance-hall peacemaker, said, 'The scariest moment I ever had doing the door was the night that all hell broke loose in the Cameo/Stardust. On this particular night, the stairs leading to the dance floor were packed with dancers. Something happened at the top of the stairs which caused the dancers to panic. Some tried to flee back down and people got crushed. The pressure on the railings caused them to buckle and people got jammed in between them. Other dancers fell on top of them and it developed into a very serious situation with people's lives at risk. I noticed John Magee was badly hurt and in some trouble so I grabbed hold of him and pulled him to safety. Others were also in a bad way, with people lying on top of them. So we just grabbed the people on top and actually threw them to safety in order to get to the people lying on the stairs. In the background, we could hear a fleet of ambulances racing to the dance hall. We were lucky nobody was too badly hurt in the end up.'

The swift decisive action of Stout and the other bouncers that night averted what could have been a tragedy. Stout then talked about how they coped with fights at some venues.

'As far as fighting was concerned, Borderland was a relatively quiet dance hall, with perhaps the Stardust being more lively in that department.

Legendary bouncer Gerald 'Stout' Ferguson with his girlfriend Frankie McGill enjoying a dance at Borderland on a rare night off.

But if truth be told, the rows were more like playground scuffles than vicious bare-knuckle fights. People only wanted a night of dancing and craic, and fighting was the furthest thing from their minds. Having said that, of course, there were a few fights over the years, but they were soon quelled by the bouncers before they got out of hand. Anyone evicted from the dance hall for fighting was normally barred for six weeks. I often smile to myself when I call to mind boys coming down to the dance-hall door and asking if their time was up yet and us telling them no, they had another week to go.'

Gerald smiles as he tells me, 'I did a bit of matchmaking at the dances as well. I remember a good friend of mine was too shy to ask this girl, now his wife, to dance. So I just grabbed him and landed him beside her and said, look, he fancies you and you like him, so away you both go out to dance.'

Gerald added: 'I was only nineteen years old when I first bounced at Borderland with my brother John and Gerry Taggart. My mentor was the incomparable Barman Duffy, so I had a good teacher. All in all, they were mostly hassle-free nights, and the odd fight was more pushing and shoving. I look back on the showband and dance-hall days with fondness and would do it all again, given the chance.'

Gerald's good friend and fellow bouncer Danny Ogle was another popular doorman in and around Derry venues. He looked back on the many challenges he faced while on the door of night clubs and bars for over thirty years.

'I faced every situation imaginable, from gang fights to family feuds, even a man toting a gun. It was all in a night's work. As Stout said, most people are very good, really, and only want a night's craic in a bar. I like to think I treat people with respect, and in return they respect me. It's as simple as that. You have to understand some people's personality may change slightly when they have had a few drinks, so you need to allow for that. There is no point in going over to a person, roaring and shouting or

Margaret McCauley sharing a joke with her charismatic beau Danny Ogle in 1970.

finger pointing, those days are long gone. A quiet word in their ear more times than not will do the trick. However, I would be lying if I didn't acknowledge it doesn't get any easier.'

Danny, a keen boxer in his younger days, says his claim to fame was becoming Ulster Heavyweight Champion. 'I will never forget that night. It was Monday 28 February 1983. As I stepped through the ropes to enter the ring, I saw this giant of a man make his entrance by jumping *over* the ropes. As the bell went, he hit me a cracker on the side of the face and my head shook. I instinctively just let fly with both hands and connected on target and he staggered backwards on the ropes. But before I could throw another punch, the referee stepped in and stopped the fight. I couldn't believe it. Back in Derry, we headed to Duffy's Bar and Hugh Duffy filled the cup. It was that big it took ten pints of beer to fill it. Everyone in the bar had a drink from it. What a night that was!'

Danny went on: 'My biggest triumph, however, was the day I convinced my wife to go out with me. It was after nearly running her down with my message bike. I was working for Stevenson's bakery and I was cycling down William Street doing a delivery. As I was coming to the zebra crossing at McLaughlin's hardware shop I noticed this girl crossing the road, so I stopped. She panicked a little, as she thought I was going to run her down and grabbed the carrier on the front of my bike. I told her not to panic, to calm herself, and she just walked on after giving me a bad look.

'She looked kind of cute, so I inquired who she was and found out she was a friend of Ann Boyle, a girl I knew. Ann told me her name was Margaret McCauley. Ann asked did I fancy her and I said yes. A few days later, Ann told Margaret this curly-haired boy was asking about her and arranged for us to meet, which we did. At first she wasn't too keen on me. But after we met on other occasions, she decided to go on a date with me. We just took it from there, and here we are today, forty-two years later.'

Just talking to Danny Ogle, you can feel his zest for life and he is never without a joke or a smile. It's easy to understand why he is so popular.

Some of the bouncers who were trusted with keeping the peace at the many dance halls in and near Derry were:

The Criterion
Paddy Bonnar, Alex Hegarty, Charlie Harkin (snr), Joe McIntyre, Tony McIntyre, Hugh Harkin, Jim McDermott, Charlie 'Ming' Harkin, Eddie McDermott.

The Embassy
John McLaren, Paddy Logue, Peter Rogers, John Payne, Hugh Payne, Leo Donohoe, Brian McCool, Paddy Brown, Patsy Loughery.

The Plaza, Buncrana
Sonny Quinn, Jim Quinn, Danny McNutt, Billy 'Spider' Kelly, Paddy Kelly, Jim Murray.

The Castle, Dungiven
Mickey Diamond, Hugh 'Boots' McCann, Patsy Loughery, Seamus 'Duncan' McCann, Patsy 'Yachts' McDermott.

The Guildhall
Jim Thornton, Jim Hockley, Paddy Kelly, 'Greta' Paddy Kerr, Red Leo Doran, Eddie McMenamin, Mickey McMenamin, Jimmy Monaghan, Joe 'Oily' McBride, Patsy Brolly.

Borderland, Corinthian, Stardust, Point Inn
Patrick 'Barman' Duffy, Gerald 'Stout' Ferguson, John Ferguson, Dick McQuade, Liam Crossan, Paddy Crossan, George Cregan, Jim McGeady, Jim 'Spud' McCready, Jim 'Spider' Kelly, Frank Stewart, Hugh Kelly, Denis Hannaway, Willie Kelly, John Morrison, Brian Breslin, Paddy McFadden, Jamesie McIntyre, Jim 'The Yank' Schwartz, Patsy Begley, Paddy Ward, Frank Ward, Davy Patterson, Len Donnelly, John Donnelly, 'Red' Jimmy Loughery, Dom Harkin, Pat Harkin, John McGinley.

The morning after the night before. Abbie McGuinness, Tommy Donnelly and Joe McCallion in Yanarelli's café on Strand Road, Derry, playing records on the jukebox in 1962.

Two Derry ladies pause for a quick photo with two visiting sailors at the Plaza in 1964.

Billy Kyle keeping a tight hold of his girlfriend Margaret Grant at the Stardust in 1967.

Good friends Maureen McGrory and Gerry Doherty share a dance at the Plaza Ballroom in 1964.

Eddie Sheils and Eileen Deery at a friend's wedding in the City Hotel a month after their own wedding in 1972.

Home alone again for Kevin Mulheron and Joe Keys, out of luck once more at the Pallidrome in Strabane in 1968.

Happy couples pictured at the Plaza in 1966. In the background is well-known Derry teacher Tommy McDermott.

Mates and muckers celebrating St Patrick's Day 1961 in the Hong Bar before heading to the Corinthian Ballroom. At the mike is 'Nanny' Reilly. Also included are Gerry Doherty, Neilly McCarron, Mike McAllister and John McCafferty.

Lila Sheerin, Billy McCauley and Vera Sheerin relaxing in the Matador Bar at Muff before heading into Borderland in 1967.

Below: The Checkers playing at a dance in the Guildhall, Derry, in 1968. Included are Seamus Downey on saxophone and Pat McCrossan with his double-necked guitar.

America Bound

While the southern showbands were now streaming towards the Derry, Donegal and Tyrone dance halls, two Derry girls were exiting the dance-hall scene here for a new life in America in the early 1960s.

Susan Doherty – or as she prefers to be called, 'Ginger' Doherty – from Creggan was another young Derry girl who was wowed by an American Navy man stationed here. She told me how she met her Michigan-born husband in the Embassy Ballroom.

Ginger Doherty and husband Gerry Hansen in Bangkok, Thailand, where they were stationed with the US Navy in 1967.

'I was at a dance with my friend Charlotte Fitzpatrick and there was this fellow there I knew who sold the *Ireland's Saturday Night* at the Guildhall. He told me that a Yank over in the corner wanted to dance with me. I told him if he wanted to dance with me, let him come over and ask me himself. Well, I didn't dance him that night, as I was asked out by someone else a minute later. The Embassy was packed and we lost sight of each other and he left my mind.

'The following week I went to the Embassy again with friends and we were sitting at a table in the balcony when I noticed the Yank coming towards us. He approached our table and asked me if I was Ann. I told him I wasn't. He didn't seem to believe me and asked if I was sure. I said, "Do you not think I know my own name?" He walked away and again he left my mind.

'Coincidentally, my sister was getting married to a Yank a couple of weeks later and I was her bridesmaid. My sister told me a fellow called Gerry Hansen was doing best man. Of course, the name didn't mean anything to me at that time. But you can imagine my surprise when I found out the best man was him!

'He actually brought a girl to the wedding with him, but he stuck by my side all day long. I told him he didn't need to stay with me and that he should go back to his girlfriend. But he refused and said it was his duty to stay in my company as I was the bridesmaid. That night he asked me out, but I told him to get lost as he had a girl with him. So he finished with her and asked me out again and this time I agreed. We were regulars at the Embassy and the Corinthian, and a few months later he proposed to me. My father refused to let me get married, as he wanted me to marry a Derryman. The fact that Gerry was a lot older than me didn't impress my father, either.

'I pleaded with my mother to persuade my father to agree to the wedding. After many discussions with my mother on the merits of me marrying an American Navy man, my father finally gave us his blessing. Gerry and my dad later became very good friends. We got married in St Mary's Church in Creggan in July 1962.

'Three days after the wedding, Gerry was posted to Philadelphia and I did not join him until October. That was the worst of times. I was feeling lonely because I knew nobody there, and to be honest, I didn't like the place at all. Still, it has fond memories for me in a way, as my two sons were born there.

'Throughout Gerry's thirty-year US Navy career we travelled the world. My children started their school days at the Holy Child School in Creggan; my two sons graduated in Iceland and my daughter graduated in the Philippines. One of my sons now lives in New York, the other lives in New Mexico and my daughter lives in California. And it had all started with a glance across the floor at a dance in the Embassy.'

Despite her worldwide travels, Ginger, now back living in Derry, said, 'I have seen the sun go down in many far-off, romantic places, but I wouldn't trade Derry for any of the places I have been to. There is definitely no place like home.'

Dancers enjoying a cuppa at the luxurious Embassy café in 1964.

The Embassy Band with Harry Harkin entertaining dancers at the Embassy in the late 1950s.

*Alma Cogan,
one of the many
international
stars to perform
at the Embassy
Ballroom, 1964.*

Mystery band and singers at the Embassy in the early 1960s.

Teenage Romance

Also about to depart the city of her birth for the shores of America was nineteen-year-old Sadie Rogers (née Gallagher) from the Brandywell.

Sitting in Sadie's comfortable living room, listening to her reminisce about her youth was not only a laugh-a-minute experience but an education. Sadie, despite all her years in America, never lost her Derry accent. She recalled with clarity and fondness the innocent antics she and her friends got up to as young girls in their early teens. Sadie began by telling how attending her first dance turned into a teenager's nightmare.

'I was fourteen and just left school. I heard my older sister Lily and some other girls talking about one of their friends who was going with this boy who was a spitting image of Robert Mitchum the film star. God, I was mad about Robert Mitchum, so I said to myself, I have to see this boy. After eavesdropping on their conversation, I knew they were meeting in the Mem the following night. The next day, I went over to Maureen McGilloway's house in Sugarhouse Lane and told her what I'd heard. So we decided we would go to the Mem that night; it would be our very first dance. Maureen was panicking in case we wouldn't be allowed in, as we were only fourteen years old. I told her if we put make-up on and doll ourselves up, we would pass for eighteen.

'But I had a problem: I was flat chested. So I got a loan of a bra from Maureen's house and stuffed it with cotton wool. I 'borrowed' our Lily's skirt and a pair of our Jenny's shoes and nylons. I told me da and ma I was going to the pictures. I looked in to the mirror as I was leaving the house and thought I was the bee's knees, as I looked all grown-up. So off we headed for the Mem, chewing gum and walking ever so proper. We got to the door of the Mem and paid our shilling and sixpence and got in, no problem. All the men were talking with a southern brogue and later I found out they were fellows from Dublin and Cork who'd joined the British Navy. We soon spotted our Lily's friend with her sailor boyfriend and, true to their word, he was the spitting image of Robert Mitchum. The only difference was he was only about five foot two. Still, he looked a wee vision.

'We started to dance beside them, and all of a sudden I felt my bra slipping. Maureen whispered to me, "Sadie, we need to go to the toilet and adjust your bra because one is three inches above the other!"

'So off we went and just as we came back with all the necessary adjustments made, I heard someone scream my name. Looking round, there was our Lily and she gave me an earful and threatened to tell my da if I didn't sit beside her all night.

No cheek-to-cheek ban here as sailors smooch around the floor with local girls at the Embassy in 1965.

*Pat McAllister, Marie McAdams, Brendan 'Bo' O'Donnell and John O'Driscoll were the
main disc jockeys at the Embassy Ballroom in the late 1960s.*

A fellow came over and asked me out to dance and Lily nearly devoured him, telling
him, "Get away! She is only a child." After the dance, I had to walk home about ten
yards in front of our Lily and her sailor boyfriend that night.

'It was about six months later that I ventured up to the Mem again with Martha
Mowbray from Newbuildings. Martha was a frequent dancer at the Mem and knew
all the ropes. We had a ball that night and I went to several more dances in the Mem
and enjoyed every one of them. But thank God my da never found out I was dancing in the Mem; he wouldn't have approved.

'Then it was the Corinthian for me. God, I really loved dancing in that hall. I
also liked the Plaza in Buncrana and loved dancing there to the Rhythm Boys. I
remember the Rhythm Boys would come up to Jenny's in McKeown's Lane after a
dance and would have a sing-along with Eddie Kerr and Stan Cauley.'

Sadie went on to tell me how she met her husband-to-be on his first night in
Derry. 'I was doing overtime with Joan Clarke in the shirt factory and after work
we decided to go to Coyle's fish-and-chip shop on Carlisle Road. We only had a few
pence between us so we sat in the stalls and ordered a bag of chips, a bottle of coke
and two straws. As we were eating, these three big Yanks came in and sat in the stall
facing us. One of them got up, came over to our stall and said, "Hi, there. I'm Stan
Rogers from Georgia in the United States."

'He was tall, tanned and very handsome. I said, "Hi to you, too. I'm Sadie Gallagher from Bridge Street." And both Joan and I started laughing. He asked if he could sit down and we said yes. Then his mates came and joined us as well. He was very well mannered and he told us he had just arrived in Derry that day. After talking to us for over an hour, they asked us if we would like to go to the pictures the next night. We agreed and had a good time and that was the start of it.

'I liked him and went out with him steady after that. Three or four months later, he pro-posed to me. I told him I would need to think about it and we continued to go out together for another year or so.'

Sadie went on: 'The Ameri-can sailors treated girls very well and were kind and considerate,

American Stan Rogers and Derry girl Sadie Gallagher on their wedding day in 1966.

and money was no object. My mother loved Stan, as he was so gentle and well man-nered, but my father, like all Derry fathers I suppose, would have preferred if I'd gone out with a Derryman.

'On one particular occasion, Stan and me were going through one of our wee tiffs and we'd broken up for a while. I was coming out of work in the Abercorn Factory and he was waiting for me with a big bunch of beautiful flowers. He handed them to me and said, "Look, let's stop this argument here and now. I want to marry you as soon as possible." We chatted and decided to set a date and get married.

'Several months later we were married in the Long Tower Church and lived in Derry for a while where we had our first child. Stan was then posted back to Amer-ica so we moved there and had another child some years later. Stan had completed several other foreign tours of duty when he came home one night and said, "I've been posted again, this time thousands of miles away." Fearing the worst, I asked him where to this time? And he just stood there in the middle of the living room with a smile on his face and said, "A place called Derry in Ireland." I jumped for joy. It was like a dream come true. We were going home again.'

The 1960s in Full Swing

The swinging '60s were now in full swing and those years saw the birth of the exciting Merseybeat sound, led by the Beatles, which captivated teenagers everywhere. They not only changed the music scene but the dress, hairstyles and lifestyles of many teenagers worldwide. Out went the Teddy Boy suits, skin-tight trousers and can-can dresses. In came the 'cool' flared trousers, cuban-heeled Beatle boots, and slick tailor-made, three-piece and double-breasted suits. Not forgetting the matching spotted tie and breast-pocket handkerchief. The fashion-conscious male teenager now also sported longer hair. The ladies favoured the miniskirt and minidresses to the pencil-thin, tight skirt or the can-can dresses.

Worldwide star Chubby Checker billed for a St Columb's Hall concert on 22 July 1963. Supporting him on the show is a host of local talent. This was Chubby Checker's first-ever appearance in Ireland.

The 1960s are regarded as the vintage years, the golden era of bands and music. With the Beatles came the Rolling Stones, the Searchers, Billy J Kramer, Manfred Mann, Tom Jones, Engelbert Humperdinck, Roy Orbison, Dickie Rock, Brendan Bowyer, Joe Dolan – the list is almost endless and their music is proving timeless. Coupled with the new Merseybeat sound we had the big brass sound of the Irish showbands. Although mainly doing cover versions, they made it a magical time, dancing-wise, in Ireland in the '60s. With the massive popularity of the showbands, Ireland was awash with not only showbands but dance halls. There was one in every city, town and village in the country. With the choice of so many dance halls in, or in close proximity to, Derry, all hosting top showbands almost on a nightly basis, this naturally gave us many options. Busloads of teenagers were ferried to and from all of these venues and it was the norm for dance halls to be packed.

The southern showbands now almost totally dominated the dance-hall scene in the whole of Ireland. The Royal, the Miami, the Drifters, the Capitol, the Dixies, and the Cadets were now joined by the likes of the Freshmen (the best showband of them all in my humble opinion), the Chessmen, the Nevada, the Arrows, and Derrick and the Sounds. These 'new' showbands were mainly pop orientated, which was more to the liking of the younger dancers. The promoters and dance-hall owners were making a lot of money as were the top showbands of the time.

Myra McGowan and Noel Barr, who have danced miles across the dance floors of many ballrooms, are seen here at the Guildhall in 1960.

Suzie Norby with her boyfriend John McCafferty during a break from dancing at the Cameo in 1965.

Childhood pals Pat McCloskey and Theresa Deery having fun at the Guildhall in 1964.

Geraldine Fletcher, Alan Wright and Sheila O'Brien enjoy listening to the band at the Embassy in April 1967.

Dickie Rock meets his number-one fan Molly Kelly with her friend Kathleen McGlinchey at the Pallidrome, Strabane, in 1963.

Dickie Rock's Number 1 Fan

Molly Kelly from the Top of the Hill in the Waterside area of Derry has been a Dickie Rock fan for close on fifty years. When asked why, she talks in glowing terms about her favourite showband star. Molly rolls off a number of reasons. 'Well, his songs are just fantastic, and he is so charismatic and a great mover on the stage. The hair on the back of my neck still stands, even to this day, when Seán Coyle plays *Every Step Of The Way* or *The Candy Store* on the wireless. I first saw Dickie in the Pallidrome in Strabane in 1963 when I went there with my friend Kathleen McGlinchey. He came off the stage after the dance was over and we chatted with him for a few minutes. We got our photograph taken with him and he was such a gentleman. From then on, I was smitten, and Dickie Rock and the Miami became my favourite showband.

'I followed them to every dance hall in or around Derry. If he was on in the Fiesta in Letterkenny, the Plaza in Buncrana, the Golden Slipper in Magilligan or the Pallidrome in Strabane, we would be there. Since that night way back in 1963 I have collected hundreds of photographs and newspaper clippings of him. Mind you, I loved Butch Moore and the Capitol as well.'

Molly went on to reminisce about the dance halls. 'I loved going to my first dance in the Corinthian in my can-can dress with my sister and friends. That night sticks out in my mind. However, as much as I liked the Corinthian, I would have to admit that Borderland was my favourite dance hall. It had an atmosphere that no other could match. I think it was because the Corinthian was mainly frequented by mostly Derry people and while it was truly great, Borderland would have had dancers from everywhere which made the atmosphere there unique. I sit here at night and think of all the fun I had with my friends at those dances all those years ago. My memories never diminish, because I still play the old showband records every night before I retire to bed. I wouldn't trade the memories of my youth, the showband years and dances for all the tea in China.'

Molly finished off by praising a local band: 'The Foyle Showband were brilliant, too, and Mickey Wilson was the best singer they ever had.'

A lot of people feel the same way as Molly about the showband years, the ballrooms of romance and the bands that played in them. The mere mention of the magical days of the showband era sends a certain age group into fits of laughter at the fond memories.

'All it took then was a twinkle of an eye across a crowded dance floor and before you knew it, you were smooching with the girl and oblivious to everyone else in the hall. After that it was *Rock Around The Clock* and soon you were doing the Hucklebuck,' roared Harry Gilmore with laughter. 'For me, the Memorial Hall was the best; I loved it. There were some great jivers in that hall. Ah, those were the days.'

'Aye, and not a drop of alcohol was sold in the dances then, either, and they attracted crowds of hundreds and sometimes thousands,' chipped in Johnny Doherty as the laughter subsided before adding, 'but to tell you the truth, I was always well tanked before I went into the dances then, anyway. And the hardest part for me was to try and walk straight as I passed Barman Duffy or Paddy Bonnar at the door.'

*One of the most popular bands to play at the Embassy were the Chessmen, with local lad
Gerry Anderson in the line-up.*

The last stop for many dancers was always Duddy's fish-and-chip shop on William Street. Dickie Rock and Fran O'Toole from the Miami Showband are enjoying the company and the food at the shop in 1968. Also included are Brendan Duddy, Bernie Mount, Neil Campbell and Kay Duddy.

Last-Chance Saloon

Frankie 'Spud' Murphy remembers most people heading home from the Embassy or Stardust or other venues who didn't 'get off' would end up in Duddy's fish-and-chip shop in William Street.

Bernadette Mount, who was manageress of Duddy's, smiles at the memory. She commented: 'You could write a book on our wee fish-and-chip shop. We made a point of staying open until the bus arrived back from Borderland, no matter how late it was. Actually, it was regarded as the last-chance saloon on a Friday or Saturday night if things didn't go to plan at the dance. The craic was always good at weekends and it was a great place to work. We would watch from behind the counter as a fellow tapped up a girl. We knew in an instant whether she would go with him or not, as the look on a man's face always tells a story. It was just the experience you gained from working there; all the girls could tell in a jiffy.

'Many got lucky when they met someone who was at a different dance to them and they could end up going home with someone. I can tell you, many a marriage emanated from our wee fish-and-chip shop in William Street,' she laughs. 'The crowds of dancers coming out of the Embassy and Borderland on a Friday night and the Stardust, Embassy and the Mem on a Saturday night turned William Street into a mini Piccadilly Square. It resembled an open meeting point and some people congregated there that were not even at a dance, just for the craic.'

93

I asked Bernie if she did much dancing herself.

'Oh, yes. I loved Borderland and I also had a liking for ballroom dancing; I entered a lot of competitions. I actually represented Northern Ireland in ballroom dancing.' Concluding, Bernie said, 'Duddy's was a part of Derry history in the sixties; many people met their life partner there. All the workers loved their time there, and we made a point every year of making a Christmas dinner for the poor street drinkers. Despite all the confrontation that took place in William Street, and even with the onslaught of the Troubles, I can say, hand on heart, we never had a minute's bother with anyone inside our wee shop. It has nothing but the happiest of memories for me and everyone who worked there. I'm delighted that the young people of the sixties and seventies remember us so fondly.'

Just as Maggie Friel's fish-and-chip shop at Rossville Street had been a famous stopping place for many of the dancers in the '50s, Duddy's in William Street followed on as a late-night drop-in centre and gathering place after the dances in the '60s. So, although the dress styles and the showbands changed, the teenagers followed similar social patterns for almost two decades.

Congratulations! These ladies have just gained a certificate of dance excellence at the Embassy, 1968.

Having a drink in Ken's Den in 1963 are David Bland from Maryland, Margaret Boyle from Tyrconnell Street, Bob Redmond from New York and Belle McColgan from Artisan Street.

From Ken's Den to California

In the 1960s there were still a lot of American and British servicemen in the city, either stationed there or on shore leave from their ships berthed at the quay. They were also frequent visitors to the dance halls of the North West where they added a bit of colour to the proceedings in many ways.

In April 1963, Bob Redmond was a happy-go-lucky young man serving with the US Navy in Newport, Rhode Island. This New York City born twenty-year-old was, however, about to have his life turned upside down when he was informed he was being transferred to Derry. Bob was excited at the prospect but he knew nothing about the city at the time. But now Derry holds a special place in his heart, because it is where he found the girl of his dreams – Belle McColgan.

Bob reminisces: 'Coming from the Big Apple, I thought Derry was quaint. The people were naturally friendly and we were treated very well everywhere we went. Complete strangers would say hello when passing you on the street – now, that's something that would never happen in New York City.'

Bob admits to being a sharp dresser in those days and recalls Derry wasn't quite ready for his cutting-edge New York City sharkskin suit with its velvet collar and cuffs. However, his wife Belle's story is slightly different. Belle, originally from Artisan Street in Rosemount, recalled: 'I told him I didn't like his suit and that he looked like a rowdy Yank dressed as a Teddy Boy. I went on to tell him if he wanted a nice suit he'd have to pay a visit to Burton's in Ferryquay Street and get himself measured for a proper one. I told him he wasn't in New York now, that he was in Derry and he'd need to dress accordingly. Obediently, Bob took my advice and the very next day, off to Burton's he went to get outfitted just like a refined Derryman.

'When he did this, I must admit, I was suitably impressed and I decided there and then this is the man I want to date, this is the man for me. But not just yet! I had a small problem to sort out: I was supposed to go on a date with his superior. I had to break the news to him first before I could go on a date with Bob. This I did straightaway and since my first date with Bob, which was way back in 1963, we have been side by side ever since.

'I remember the first night I met him. I was working at that time as a beautician and hairdresser and was visiting a client, Peggy Gallagher, at her husband's pub, Ken's Den at the top of Carlisle Road. Peggy was quite busy working behind the bar and she asked me to carry a round of drinks down to a table. Bob was there with his friend, also from the American base, who was going out with Peggy's sister Cathy. Bob asked Cathy to introduce us and she did. He then asked me for a date and we went for a meal the next night – after I finished with his superior – to the Chinese restaurant on Shipquay Street. After the meal, we went to the Strand cinema to see the midnight matinée.

'A couple of weeks later, Bob arrived to collect me for a date in his new suit. He was wearing a three-piece black wool suit with scarlet lining! When I saw him, I just shook my head and threw my arms in the air, thinking to myself that this young man needs a bit more work. To make matters worse, his two mates had the same identical tailor-made suits. After a bit more prompting, I finally got him sorted out and we were as happy as Larry after that.

Bob Redmond (centre) and fellow Navy personnel attend a memorial service in the Waterside Church for President Kennedy in November 1963.

Bob Redmond and Belle McColgan on their wedding day at St Eugene's Cathedral in 1965 with Fr Edward Daly and best man Paddy Callan and bridesmaid Helen Downey.

'About eighteen months later, on 26 August 1965, we were married in St Eugene's Cathedral by Father Daly. At first we lived in a flat at Magazine Street. The following year, Bob was transferred to Newport, Rhode Island. That was the beginning of our world travels. He was transferred to Bainbridge in Maryland and then to Mare Island and Treasure Island in California. Next we were based in the beautiful Pacific island of Hawaii where we lived for ten glorious years.

'Our last overseas posting was Puerto Rico. By then, Bob was promoted to Senior Chief Petty Officer and we were transferred back to Charleston, South Carolina, where we eventually settled. Bob may have come all the way to Derry for me, but then I had to follow him halfway round the world,' laughs Belle.

Belle admits arriving in America was a culture shock and she missed Derry terribly for a long time.

'I cried every day and longed for my family, my friends and my lovely neighbours from Rosemount. And when Bob was at sea for months on end it was lonely and that was the worst time. But when my two daughters were born they kept me busy; all my time was taken up caring for them. And then you had the other sailors' wives to keep you company and they were all so friendly. Fortunately, there were always a

97

Advert from the Derry Journal, *April 1965.*

few Derry girls living everywhere we were assigned. Even though I never knew them when I lived in Derry, we soon became close and we are now lifelong friends. Margaret Glenn from the Lone Moor Road lives very close to us as does Dinah Nash from Rosemount. We are also very close friends with Margaret Boyle and her husband, with whom we still maintain contact and visit in their home whenever we can. Margaret is from Tyrconnell Street and has also been in America for a long time.'

Belle then reminisced about her dancing days and the first ballroom she went to.

'My friend Annie McDaid and I went to the Crit in Foyle Street when we were only fourteen. I still laugh when I think of me and my friends taking our first faltering steps into our teenage dancing years. While dancing cheek-to-cheek, the mixture of perspiration and hairspray would cause our faces to become almost stuck together by the end of the dance.

'We enjoyed it so much that we danced two or three nights a week in different halls. From the Corinthian one night to the Embassy another night and then, like everybody else, we danced at Borderland. I loved the showbands; how could we forget them! Johnny Quigley was my favourite, but the Royal and the Clipper Carlton were also very good. Annie and myself still talk about all those happy times we had at the dances back then.'

Bob concluded by saying, 'When I first saw Belle I thought she was the loveliest girl I'd ever seen and I still think that today. Marrying her was the best thing I have ever done in my life and I still make a point of bringing her home flowers once or twice a week.'

Although Belle and her daughters have been regular visitors to Derry over the years, Bob has never returned since the day he left with his new bride way back in 1966, but he hopes to enjoy our shores again soon.

Bob and Belle have two beautiful daughters and three lovely grandchildren. They live a comfortable and happy life in sun-drenched Goose Creek, which is a picturesque suburb of Charleston, South Carolina. However, as far as Belle is concerned, Derry is, and will always be, home to her.

Again having a drink, but this time in California in 2009, are David and Margaret Bland, now married forty-six years, and Bob Redmond and Belle McColgan, now married forty-seven years.

Margaret Follows Her Heart

Belle's husband Bob was a close pal of David Bland who was also stationed at the American base in Derry in the early 1960s. David also met and fell in love with a Derry girl, Margaret Boyle from Tyrconnell Street. Both couples socialised together in Derry before they married and their friendship is as strong today as it was back in 1963.

Margaret was a keen dancer in her teenage years and remembers the first dance she attended was at the Ritz Hall, just off the Strand Road. 'I went with Helen Kelly who lived across the street from me; she now lives in Connecticut. I was still at school and worked at the Rainbow café for a few hours each day after school and on a Saturday just to get the money to go to the dances. I remember I had a wile notion of this wee fellow – we were only about fifteen. At a dance in the Ritz one night I saw him walking towards me and he took me out to dance and my wee heart was racing. I can still remember the song that was being played as we danced; it was *Save The Last Dance For Me*, the big Drifters hit. It is still one of my favourite songs, and even with the passing of so many years, those teenage memories never seem to fade.

'On leaving school I followed my sisters and went to work in the City Factory. I went to most of the dances with my friends Helen Kelly, Clare Bridge from the old Bogside – when it was only one street – and Ann Duffy from Rossville Street. We loved dancing and we went everywhere: Borderland, the Corinthian, the Embassy, the Guildhall and even up to the Pallidrome in Strabane. They all had their own special atmosphere, but I would have to say Borderland was our favourite dance hall. It was the hub of excitement, as all the bigger showbands played there. Brendan Bowyer and the Royal was our favourite showband. Bowyer had so much charisma and was so energetic that his enthusiasm swept down to the dancers on the dance floor. The atmosphere there was just fantastic and we just lived for the weekends. We also had an affinity with the Corinthian Ballroom and it was there that I first saw a superstar live on stage: Billy Fury. I also remember the night Acker Bilk came to the Guildhall and some big names coming to the Embassy.

THE NEVADA with ROLY DANIELS & KELLEY

MANAGER - TOMMY HAYDEN, WINDER PLACE, GREYSTONES, CO. WICKLOW. PHONE 874753.

'It was while dancing in the Corinthian that I met my husband David Bland from Chestertown, Maryland. He was a serving US sailor stationed at their Clooney Road base. Dave had known my sister Lola for quite a while before I met him. My sister just happened to be there and Dave was talking to her and saw me on the dance floor. He obviously noticed me because he asked her if she knew me. She then introduced us and we started going out together shortly after that. While going steady, we would normally go to the Corinthian or just to the pictures or up to Ken's Den for a quiet drink.

'Dave left Derry in October 1964 for a new tour of duty to Washington DC. I followed on 28 December of the same year to Maryland, to Dave's family home. We married in Dave's hometown of Chestertown, Maryland, in April 1965. Unfortunately, my family was unable to attend our wedding because of the distance and the cost of travel. We lived in Washington DC where Dave was stationed. I travelled many miles following Dave to his many postings: to Midway Island, San Diego, Norfolk, Virginia and Baltimore, to name but a few.'

When asked did she often feel homesick, Margaret replied, 'I broke my heart and cried daily if I heard a song on the radio or television that would remind me of Derry; I would just burst into tears. Often, when Dave was at work and the children at school, I would sit down, close my eyes and pretend I was walking over Rossville Street, down William Street and into Waterloo Place and up the town. I was homesick from the day I left our wee terrace home in Tyrconnell Street.'

Dave recalls he was actually in Derry by default, as he only put Ireland on his duty request form because he thought there was no base in Ireland and he really wanted to go to sea.

'I was originally assigned to Derry for eighteen months but I enjoyed my time here so much that I extended my enlistment so I could stay for another twelve months. But when I first came to Derry, it was nothing like I thought it would be. I knew very little about Ireland except what I saw in the movies, which was not very much. However, I soon grew to like Derry, as its people were very friendly and nice to talk to; they were good listeners as well.

'Before I met Margaret, I would go with my mates to the Embassy, Borderland and the Corinthian. If we were just going out for a drink, we normally would go to the Diamond Bar, the Rocking Chair or the Telstar up in Creggan. I loved eating at Fiorentini's fish-and-chip shop, the Savoy and the Sailors' Rest.'

I asked Dave as to his thoughts why they were so popular with the girls.

'I suppose we were viewed as a novelty and offered better opportunities for the local girls. I grew up in a small town with a population of around five thousand people and the same happened there. On the outskirts there was an army base with about a hundred and fifty soldiers stationed there. Their only chance of female companionship was the local girls. The girls loved the attention, but the local guys didn't appreciate the invasion and at times showed it with the odd fight breaking out.'

Margaret and Dave have four sons and grandchildren and live in retirement just a few miles from Orlando, Florida. They have been back to Derry on a few occasions and Margaret says, 'I had a wonderful mother and father and a very happy upbringing in Derry. We were a close-knit family and I have nothing but the fondest of memories of my childhood and teenage days in Derry. I was blessed to have had such lovely friends and neighbours in our wee street. Still to this day when I return home and catch the first glimpse of the Foyle the tears will roll down my cheeks.'

Margaret and husband Dave still, after forty-five years, remain close friends with Belle and Bob and other Derry girls who became wives of American Navy personnel. Although they may live many hundreds of miles apart, Belle and Bob visit Margaret and Dave in their Florida home as often as possible. It's uncanny when you look at the two different photographs which were taken forty-five years apart. Not only are they sitting side by side, but in the same sequence, one taken in Ken's Den in Derry in the '60s and the other in America in 2010. Both men stressed the point that the Americans who married Derry brides all those years ago still keep in touch. And the strong bond between them is certain to continue through the reunions that take place every year organised by the Derry Navcommsta Alumni Association.

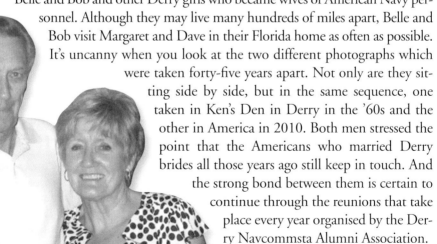

Dave and Margaret at their home in California, 2011.

Liam Fleming and friend at the Plaza in 1966.

Christine Magill with her husband Jamesie Nicholl, former Coleraine and Finn Harps captain, on their wedding day in 1977. When asked why he didn't play for his hometown club, Derry City, he replied, 'Because they didn't ask me!'

Before going on to a dance in the Corinthian, Lena McCourt and a friend visit Ken's Den in 1965.

Mary McConnell and Dan Coyle at a dance in the Plaza Ballroom in 1965.

Veronica Deehan and friends take a break from dancing at the Plaza, Buncrana, in 1966.

Liam Boyle with his girlfriend Margaret McDowell at the Plaza in 1965.

Joe Heaney and girlfriend Lily Mooney at the Stardust in 1970.

Having a drink before going on to a dance are John Gibbons, Kathleen Moran, Noel McLaughlin, Terry Doherty, Kathleen Anderson, Tony Quigley, Rose Curran, Barney Moran, Harry Hamill and Theresa Young in 1965.

The Best Laid Plans . . .

While researching for this book, as you would expect, I came across a lot of lovely romantic stories from the showband and dance-hall days. However, there was one that didn't have a happy ending, despite much elaborate planning.

Through various contacts I was introduced to a man who lived overseas with a fascinating story to tell of his dance-hall days in Derry. He wished to remain anonymous and other names have been changed in this account for obvious reasons.

'It was Friday afternoon after work. I took my mucky boots off at our front door in Creggan, scrubbed them down and placed them in a plastic bag that my ma handed me. I thought the next time I would see them would be at half past seven on Monday morning. However, there was a lot of living to do before then. My mind wandered to the girl I saw every morning on the bus as I went to work. She was a wee beauty and I thought she was giving me the eye. Well, I was hoping she was. She lived in Creggan, but I didn't know where. That Friday morning I had heard her telling her mate she was going to see Eileen Reid and the Cadets in Borderland that night. I couldn't stand that band myself, but if I thought I'd get the chance to dance her or to tap her up, sure I'd go, even if the devil himself was playing.

'I remember thinking all I have to do now is to convince my mates Liam and Johnny to come with me to Borderland. Liam would be no problem, but Johnny was in a bit of a rut since Angela Sweeney had given him the elbow three weeks previously. I took a bath and had a wee lie-down on the bed and thought about what I would say to her while I was dancing with her. I had it all planned out in my head: I would ask her to dance, a fast dance first, and I would appear calm and cool. Then a couple of dances later, I'd make my move and ask her out on a slow dance and if all went well, ask her to go for a mineral with me. My mind then turned to what I'd wear. I decided it had to be my best three-piece suit and shirt with matching tie and pocket handkerchief and the gold cuff links I keep for special occasions.

'I decided to have just two pints, as I didn't want her to smell the drink on my breath. I convinced Liam and Johnny to go to Borderland. We got a taxi from the Rocking Chair to Muff early enough and went into the Squealing Pig for a few jars, you know, the normal routine.

'Entering Borderland, I gazed around the hall to see if I could spot her and my heart sank when I saw she wasn't there. I was beginning to feel really disappointed, because if she didn't come I'd have to listen to the Cadets for two full hours. Then I saw her strolling up the floor with two friends. She looked a really lovely girl; I didn't say anything to Liam or Johnny about her, just in case she shot me down.

Eileen Reid and the Cadets, a popular Dublin showband in the 1960s.

The crowd was just perfect, not too big not too small; everything was going to plan so far.

'Fifteen minutes later I suggested to my mates we should dance the three of them. They agreed and I led the way and asked her to dance; it was a fast one. We seemed to get on well and we engaged in small talk. I was biding my time and patiently waiting before making my move. The time was now right, I thought, and I decided to go for it. I was about six feet away from her when, all of a sudden, out of nowhere, Johnny appeared and tapped her on the arm and took her out to dance. I couldn't believe it! I was furious. All I could do was stand there and watch them smooching around the Borderland floor. I told myself to stay calm and make sure to be first over to her for the next dance. Looking at them laughing, I was beginning to get worried that they were getting on too well. The dance ended and to my horror, they just stood there in the middle of the dance floor, talking. And when the band started up a fast set, they started to jive.

'When that dance was over I was gutted when Johnny was walking her towards the mineral bar where they sat down. I was dumbfounded. A couple of minutes later I saw her getting up and making her way to the toilet. I dived over to Johnny and asked him what the craic was and he told me he was leaving her home. I couldn't believe it. The man I forced to go to the dance had wiped my eye. I decided to say nothing and when Liam and myself called for Johnny the following night he told us he had a date with her and was taking her to the Embassy.

'I was flabbergasted but decided as there was nothing I could do about it, I might as well try and enjoy myself at the Embassy. Three months later, they were still going out together and by now were visiting each other's homes. The following year, they got engaged, and one night Johnny came to my house and told me they were getting married and asked me to be his best man. I was all chuffed at that and on their wedding day, I could do nothing but quietly reflect on what might have been. To this day, they and everyone else are oblivious to my thoughts and plans on that Friday night in Borderland all those years ago.

'I left Derry a short while after the wedding in the pursuit of employment and met a lovely person to whom I was married to for thirty-five glorious years. We have four beautiful children and seven grandchildren, but unfortunately, God took her from me a few years ago. I am happy and contented now in the full knowledge we will meet again in another life.

'I have been in exile now for over forty-one years in various countries. I lead a different life entirely to the one I would have led if I had stayed in Derry. Would I have had a happier life if my youthful plan way back then had worked out? Only the Man above knows the answer to that, but somehow I really doubt it.

'Still, I wonder what they are doing tonight?'

Closed Down for Lent

The dance halls and marquees situated just over the border were booming in the '50s, '60s, and early '70s. Derry was surrounded by them: Borderland in Muff, the Fiesta in Letterkenny, the Plaza in Buncrana, and the Bridgend marquee to name but a few. There was, however, one major weak point in the southern dance-hall calendar and it lasted more than six weeks of each year – Lent. With the Catholic Church holding such sway in the Free State, many musicians were effectively made redundant as the southern dance halls were forced to close down en bloc for forty nights from Shrove Tuesday, with St Patrick's Day the only exception.

A lot of the southern dance-hall owners, and indeed the dancers themselves, had strongly held views on this subject. It was their opinion that because of the influence of the Church, their lives were being adversely affected by the closure of the dance venues.

However, the season of Lent led to a boom time for the northern dance halls, which, in the main, remained open during that time. Paddy Cole, a stalwart in the Capitol Showband, remembers that era well, and he had this to say on the subject. 'It was not as bad for some of the border bands, as they got some gigs in the North, but dancing in the twenty-six counties was simply banned. St Patrick's night was one of the biggest nights of the year, with practically every showband in the entire country out playing, as they were in big demand and everywhere was open that night.

Happy dancers flocking to the Plaza after Lent in 1963.

The Clipper arrive in Las Vegas to start their international tour.

'But most of the showbands travelled to England and some of the bigger bands even went to the USA. It was great, as we got to meet up with the other bands that were working around England and Scotland during Lent.' He smiled when he said, 'Ah, how times have changed. Imagine telling people today they wouldn't be allowed to go dancing during Lent.'

Eamonn Monaghan, the Capitol Showband keyboard player, adds, 'We were lucky to be afforded the opportunity to go to America during that time. Many other bands unfortunately found themselves out of work, which was sad, as they had families to support.'

Roseanna Sheerin and her sister Lila doing last-minute messages on a Saturday afternoon with hair in perms, looking forward to a night's dancing in the Stardust in 1967.

The Capitol found they were as popular in America as they were at home. He went on to say, 'When we went on tour in the States, there were thousands of people waiting to welcome us at Kennedy Airport. This was a time when Irish people couldn't get home, as air fares were so expensive then. We brought a little bit of Ireland out to them and I suppose we created that all-important connection with home for a lot of emigrants.'

The Memorial Hall

The Memorial Hall in Society Street, more commonly known as The Mem, was one northern dance venue that wasn't affected by Lent. Regarded as a Protestant hall, it was also very popular with some dancers of a nationalist persuasion. Actually, one of Derry's best-known jivers, Harry Gilmore, was a Saturday-night regular at the famous old dance hall. The venue drew large crowds throughout the year with dances on Saturday and Monday nights.

Two of the more popular bands that played there were the Flingels and the Woodlanders. The Flingels' lead singer, Trevor Keys, who also played bass, was regarded as one of Derry's finest ballad singers. His renditions of some of the big ballads of the time were at least equal to any of the top showband singers of the day. The band also boasted arguably one of Ireland's best drummers in Jim Whiteside, and with talented musicians like Mervyn Cargill, Liam Smith, Ronnie Ramsey, Roy Arbuckle and Johnny Nicholl, it was no wonder they proved so popular with the dancers.

The Woodlanders were also a superb band who often graced the Mem. Their leader, Tommy Crockett, secured the services of Ivan Loughlin, Ray Hetherington, Alan Wright, Mickey Wells and drummer Jackie Graham in the original line-up. Later, Billy Haslett and Alan Peoples joined as some left the band. Their talent was soon noted by some high-powered and influential people in the entertainment business and it came as no surprise when popular local businessman Bob Ferris was unveiled as their manager. They became much sought-after locally and were playing all over the North West. And everywhere they played it was usually to sell-out crowds.

Drummer Jackie Graham relayed to me how much they all enjoyed their days in the Woodlanders.

'The craic was mighty and we were a very close-knit band; we were all friends and gelled well together. We were in an envious position because we were getting paid for doing something we would gladly have done for nothing. Those were fun-filled days. Even practice nights were

great and the camaraderie among the lads was second to none. No doubt about it, they were among the best years of my life, and I look back with nothing but sheer happiness on those days in the Mem.'

Mickey Wells, another band member now living in Bath, England, told me that the Woodlanders were a big part of his teenage years.

'When we were playing in the Mem on a Saturday night, the week before the dance we were all on a high. We would rehearse for about two hours three nights a week and always made sure to have a few new numbers on our programme. It was a good way of keeping us on our toes and of stopping our show getting stale. I remember one particular song the dancers at the Mem never failed to request. It was an old Hank Thompson song, *The Wild Side Of Life*, and Ivan Loughlin would always oblige them and sing it. Many of the old Mem crowd still remember us playing that song to this day.'

Les Thompson's face glows bright red as he slowly moves his head from side to side and breathes a sigh when I mention the Memorial Hall to him.

'Boy, we had some great nights in that hall. I mostly enjoyed them from the stage as I was always playing,' said Les, a veteran of many showbands. 'Did you know it was the very first dance hall Seán Coyle ever went to?'

He recalls the fun he had when playing with the famous Donegal musical family the Ponsonbys' Blue Glows Showband.

'They were a great family and so musically gifted. I was over the moon when I got the opportunity to join them. Unlike some of the showbands, I can honestly say we never had an angry word between us. It

A black-haired and slim Les Thompson pictured with the multitalented Blue Glows Showband from Letterkenny.

was laughter all the way as we journeyed to the dance halls, played on stage and journeyed back to our homes in the middle of the night. My time with them was among the best years, musically speaking, in my life.

'People of our age were very lucky, because we had so many choices in regard to dance halls and showbands, and all within a few miles of our home. Also, the dance floors were spacious and many couples could jive with complete freedom of movement, not like the postage-stamp size of the dance floors of today.

'Those were the days when I had black hair and a slim waist line,' he chuckles before concluding. 'Ah, sure time nor tide waits for no man, and time can change a lot of things, but our memories are our own and nothing or nobody can take them from us. The memories of the dance halls and the showbands are forever etched in our minds and hearts for evermore.'

The Flingels Bandshow were always very popular in the Memorial Hall. Pictured are Trevor Keys, Jim Whiteside, Ronnie Ramsey, Liam Smith, Mervyn Cargill and Johnny Nicholl.

The Woodlanders Showband who achieved cult status at the Memorial (Mem) Hall in the 1960s. Included are Mickey Wells, Alan Peoples, Jackie Graham, Ivan Loughlin, Tommy Crockett and Raymond Hetherington. Inset are Alan Wright and Billy Hazlett, who joined the band at a later date.

Jeanette Warke, one of the city's most respected community leaders, goes into a fit of laughing when asked to describe the tentative steps towards her first dance in the Memorial Hall.

'Where do you want me to start?' she asks, her two hands cupping her face. 'Well, I started work in the Maypole grocery store in Ferryquay Street. I was plain Jeanette McBride from Belview Avenue and just turned fourteen. That very week, my older sister, who was working in Welch Margetson, 'borrowed' some nice shirt cloth from the factory.

'With that cloth, my mother made me a nice can-can skirt and a wee matching top to go with it to wear to my very first dance in the Mem. When I tried the new clothes on for the first time, I really thought I was the bee's knees. Come nine o'clock, when it was time to put my make-up on, I was really excited. I didn't spare the Pagan perfume; I was fourteen and I was out to make an impression at this, my first dance.

'I felt all grown-up as I entered the main hall in the Mem with my two friends Sylvia Stewart and Margaret Hawkins. I remember thinking to myself I was too old now for courting behind the garages at Maureen Avenue. And anyway, those boys didn't know how to kiss a girl right; they were just mouth washers!

'The first boy I went with from the dances was Ross Gallagher from the Fountain, a lovely, humble wee fellow. We went out a couple of times; he now lives in Scotland. Then I went with Gregory Scott and he went off to Australia. God, I wonder if they left to get away from me,' she roars with laughter.

'I also went with a nice fellow called Paddy Brown, but that romance was doomed from the start because Paddy was a Catholic and I was a Protestant. My mother, when she found out, told me that Granny Moore would have a fit if she knew I was going out with a Catholic. It

Jeanette McBride with soon-to-be husband and lifetime best friend David Warke in 1961.

seems she would have been put out of the Orange Order if it became known. Back in those days, we couldn't have that, so I had to finish with Paddy.

'As I was getting older, I progressed to getting my mother to perm my hair like all the older girls. Soon, I was off to Woolworth's to buy a Tweedy Twink perm and my mother would do my hair. In those days, we would join a club and pay up weekly for new clothes. I remember I used to get a new outfit maybe twice a year from Hill's shop that way.'

Jeanette says she will always remember her days in the Memorial Hall. 'It was the highlight of any teenager's week. Our normal ritual on a Saturday was to go up the town and buy some wee small item of clothing, which we would wear that night, or maybe just a different colour tube of lipstick. God, those were innocent days then.' And to emphasise that point, Jeanette went on to say: 'At ten-thirty every Saturday night in the Mem, Robert McClean, the caretaker, would come onto the stage and announce, "It's half past ten and anyone wishing to catch the last bus would need to leave soon."

'Then on a Sunday night, like everyone else, we would walk up and down Carlisle Road, which was the in-thing then. It was during one of those nights that I met the love of my life, the man who was to become my husband and my best friend.

'This particular Sunday night, as I was walking up Carlisle Road with my friends, I noticed this fellow standing in a doorway with his mate. What caught my attention was he had lovely, blond curly hair, and was wearing a white shirt and a beautifully tailored cut suit. He looked really handsome. I couldn't but notice him and as we passed him, he smiled at me and it nearly took my breath away. We walked a bit more before turning to walk back up again. As we got to the doorway in which they were standing, he said hello and started to chat to me. After talking for about an hour, he asked me for a date and I agreed to go with him to the pictures the following night. His name was David Warke and from that night on we started going steady and became inseparable. We danced everywhere together, went to every picture house in Derry. We loved jiving and because we went to so many dances we became very good jivers. We danced at the Mem, Borderland, the Stardust, the Corinthian and the Guildhall. We just followed the music and we enjoyed every single minute of it.'

Tears welled up in her eyes and her voice broke slightly as she told me of their favourite showband, the Clipper Carlton.

'Our favourite song was *The Swallow* and they always sang it so beautifully.' A smile came to her face once again as she said, 'We danced around Borderland in unison to the Clipper playing that song; it was as if we were the only two dancers on the floor.' Shaking her head as she looked me in the eyes, she told me: 'That feeling I felt while dancing around Borderland to that song with David will never leave me, never. We got married in St Columb's Cathedral on 29 July 1963 and we enjoyed a very happy life as man and wife.'

The Statesiders Showband Tragedy

It was early Saturday morning on 21 November 1964 as I, with my friend and workmate Brendan Wilkinson, walked between the huts of Springtown Camp on our way to catch the bus to Derry to work. We were first-year apprentice bricklayers working for Frank O'Connor's builders who were building St Brecan's school at the Top of the Hill in the Waterside. We were in a happy, jovial mood, as it was Saturday morning and we finished work at midday with the rest of the weekend off.

The ill-fated Statesiders Showband.

Ten minutes later we were boarding an open-back lorry at Chamberlain Street that would take us to the building site and everyone was busy with small talk. When the lorry arrived at the site we noticed a group of workmen gathered around the office area. This was unusual, because among them was John Kelly. He was 'the mixer man' who normally started fifteen minutes earlier than the rest of us. This, of course, allowed him to have the mortar ready so that the rest of the workers could start building as soon as we arrived on site.

Showband men Patsy Durnin and Gerry Mallett relaxing in 1963.

As I climbed off the back of the lorry, I could see his face was ashen white; it was then I knew something was badly wrong. He soon blurted out the awful news of an accident that had happened in the middle of the night up the country in a place called Cloughmills in County Antrim. It involved the Statesiders Showband, whose members were mainly from the Waterside area.

John went on to tell us that six young men were killed while returning home from playing at a dance. His words were etched with emotion as he relayed to us the dreadful news that four of the men killed were brothers. They were the Mallett brothers: James, Bill, Jackie and Jerry, sons of Mr and Mrs William Mallett from the Waterside. The other men killed in this horrific accident were Daniel McLaughlin and William Harrison.

Four of the men who died were married with a total of eleven children among them. The musicians of the city, and indeed the whole country, were in shock. The funerals of the young men were the largest ever seen in Derry as thousands lined the route. Businesses and schools closed for the day in sympathy. The workers of Monarch Electric turned up in their hundreds and were accompanied by the general management. Showband members from everywhere were present at the funerals. The grief of the musical fraternity was profound and the memory of that sad night is still felt by them to this day. The families had lost their loved ones; Derry had lost six of its sons.

That fateful, dark day was surely the worst in the long history of Derry showbands. Derry was a city in mourning that weekend and a cloud hung over the dance halls for weeks after that.

The Statesiders Showband never reformed.

Sheila O'Brien and Raymond McGlinchey enjoying a jive at the Plaza in 1965.

The Jokers Showband.

Derry Showband in Exile

At the peak of the showband era, there were well over 500 bands playing across Ireland. However, with the increasing popularity of the southern bands, the Derry bands were having a tough time in securing bookings.

One well-known musician commented: 'The main reason for this was that the southern showbands were now being backed and managed by the most influential people in the entertainment industry in Ireland. Those people held all the aces, they controlled everything and they used their power to maximum effect. They had on their books the most popular showbands in the country. And if a dance-hall owner wanted to book one of their superstar showbands, they had to also book a lesser-known showband that they also managed. This, of course, meant very few dates were left in the year for the dance-hall owner to fill. An example of this was that all the bigger showbands played Borderland on a Friday night while the lesser-known showbands played on a Sunday night. This near monopoly by the southern managements was to have a detrimental effect on the Derry showbands.'

Johnny Quigley All Stars, the Woodchoppers, the Barristers and Flingels were among a few of the Derry showbands who were able to continue in business, despite the emergence of the massively popular southern showbands. But the Woodchoppers were about to suffer a near fatal blow when their charismatic front man, the popular Dickie McManus, and other members of the band decided to quit the Irish circuit and emigrate to the USA in April 1965.

Dickie returned to Derry for the Christmas holidays that year and went to hear his old showband playing in Donegal. Playing lead guitar that night for the Woodchoppers was teenage sensation Colum Arbuckle, who even at such a tender age was considered a top-notch musician. Arbuckle's talent didn't go unnoticed by Dickie

116

McManus, who immediately offered him a job with his new showband in America. Touring America appealed to Colum and he told McManus that he would sleep on it overnight and give him an answer the next day.

After discussing the offer with his parents, Colum contacted McManus and told him he would be delighted to accept his offer. Dickie, who already had Em Dillon, Jackie Coyle, Mickey Murray and John Deehan on board, considered Colum the last piece in the jigsaw. He now had a showband of substance, plus the fact that he not only was surrounded by top-class musicians but all were from Derry and well known to each other. This, of course, made the line-up perfect – in every sense. They named the band (which was really a Derry band in exile) the Emerald Showband.

Colum remembers: 'I arrived on a Thursday and played my first gig with them the following night in Canada.'

Their music may have been the same as they played in the Derry dance halls, but travelling arrangements were somewhat different from what they had encountered in Ireland. Gone was travelling on the wee, winding country roads that led to a barn-like ballroom in remote rural Ireland. Now they were travelling on highways to some of the major cities of the world. Places like Chicago, New York, Boston and the main venues in Canada. Colum

The Emerald Showband, New York, was really a Derry showband in exile. Featured are Dickie McManus, John Deehan, Em Dillon, Colum Arbuckle, Jackie Coyle and Mick Murray in 1966.

A name change. Now called the Irish Revolution, Dickie McManus, Em Dillon, Jackie Coyle, Colum Arbuckle and Mick Murray in 1972.

117

recalls some of the gigs would entail round trips in excess of 2,000 miles and take two days on the road to get to the gig.

However, they now were performing in state-of-the-art ballrooms, using up-to-date modern amplification and changing in plush, centrally heated dressing rooms. It sure was a different scene to the tin-roofed ballrooms and changing in their van. The difference was stark as they went from playing in rural-Ireland ballrooms to playing in the world-famous Waldorf Astoria in New York.

They became a tremendous hit with their exiled Irish countrymen

The Clancy Brothers show off their Arans!.

all over America and Canada. Not only were they now performing in major venues, they were regularly appearing on several television shows.

Colum chuckles when he recalls the night he had to prove his versatility. 'This particular night, the famed Irish folk group Tommy Makem and the Clancy Brothers were on the same show as us and one of the brothers suddenly took ill. Panicking, they came and asked me to stand in for him. So I donned the famous white Aran sweater and became one of the Clancy Brothers for a night.'

Colum went on: 'The Emerald Showband, which hadn't had a single disagreement for the five or so years we were together, suddenly broke up when John Deehan decided to leave the band. There then followed a dispute about who actually owned the Emerald Showband name. The other five of us decided to stay together and changed the band's name to the Irish Revolution, and again we were very successful on the American circuit.'

Colum Arbuckle and Em Dillon returned home in 1972. They teamed up with Em's brother Dessie and drummer Jim Whiteside in a group called the Marksmen and played in the local bars and halls in Derry. Actually, I can now 'out' them as the culprits who introduced the cover charge to the bars in Derry. Colum explains: 'It was difficult to get the right money from bar owners for a four-piece band, so we came up with the idea of a cover charge to supplement our fee; the admission at the door was a nominal ten pence. The expected uproar from the customers followed, but as the band's reputation was so good, the customers relented and paid the ten pence. Other bands followed suit and soon a cover charge for bands playing in the bars became normal. It also became normal for people to go and hear them and have a drink before heading to the main dance halls.'

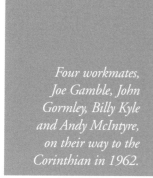

Four workmates, Joe Gamble, John Gormley, Billy Kyle and Andy McIntyre, on their way to the Corinthian in 1962.

With bookings now being few and far between for the Derry showbands, some of the musicians had a big decision to make. The success of the Emerald Showband in America prompted some of them to follow their example and take the same route. Creggan's Pat McCrossan, famous for his double-necked guitar, is still performing all over Arizona. Chuck McGuigan, Paddy Helferty, Mickey McFadden, Richard Duffy and many more left these shores to ply their music skills overseas. The Trend Showband also enjoyed success in Canada, but maybe to their detriment on the Irish showband scene.

Dickie McManus, who entertained the Derry dancers from the late 1950s until the mid-'60s in all the local dance halls, died in 2003 in Boston, Massachusetts. His death was mourned in Derry by all those who were privileged to hear him sing with the Woodchoppers Showband.

The late, great Dickie McManus.

*The Dubliners
playing for a
packed house in
the Embassy in the
mid-1960s.*

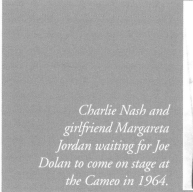

Charlie Nash and girlfriend Margareta Jordan waiting for Joe Dolan to come on stage at the Cameo in 1964.

GI Dreams Forgotten

Another Derryman who was on his way to the land of opportunity was Charlie Nash. Charlie, at the tender age of sixteen, decided to follow in his brother's footsteps and emigrate to America. He left his home in Eglinton Place in the Bogside in 1962 to go and live with him in New York.

A year or so later, Charlie came home to Derry for a holiday but fully intended to return to America in a couple of weeks. It was while he was at his mother's house that he was introduced to Margareta Jordan by his cousin and he was instantly impressed. When Margareta left to go home to the Waterside he followed her. Charlie said, 'I approached her and asked her for a date. She agreed. The next night we were sitting in the picture house, eating sweets. That weekend, I took Margareta to hear Joe Dolan and the Drifters at the Cameo. Any aspirations I had of being an American GI were suddenly way down my priority list.

'Margareta worked in Gault's shop at the bottom of Sackville Street and I used to walk her home every night. From then on, it was the same as with all other courting couples: pictures on a Monday night and dancing at the weekends, as we were now going steady. I remember taking Margareta to see Roy Orbison in the Cameo. Even though it was ten shillings per ticket – big money back then – he was well worth it. He was better than brilliant; he was magic, a class act.'

Charlie recalls that his preferred dance hall was the Guildhall, as he thought the acoustics were by far the best of any venue in the town.

'I wasn't a keen dancer then; I just preferred to listen to the bands while Margareta danced with her mates. There was one song I absolutely loathed: it was *The Hucklebuck*. Whenever a band played it, I usually disappeared to the toilet.'

Margareta, whose favourite dance hall was Borderland, said, 'I soon put a stop to Charlie not dancing and after a few nights, I couldn't keep him off the floor.'

Two years later, they were married in the Waterside Church. After their honeymoon they, like most other newlyweds at the time, lived in a room in the family home of the bride. To this day, they still love getting out at the weekend for a dance.

Charlie Nash and Margareta Jordan on their wedding day, 9 May 1967.

Majella Brady enjoying a showband dance with lifelong pal Aurora O'Brien at the Pallidrome in Strabane in 1967.

Majella on the Move

Teenage singing sensation Majella Brady was another Derry artist who decided to move away from her native Derry.

Born and reared in Corporation Street, the star of television and radio remembers fondly the very first time she was asked to sing. 'I was a wee girl of four and I was asked by a neighbour to sing a wee song. I agreed and they promptly stood me on a chair in the middle of their living room and asked me to sing *Saint Theresa Of The Roses*. Afterwards, they gave me a penny. From that day on, whenever my aunts or uncles visited our house, they would ask me to sing and they, too, would give me money for sweets. So I suppose, by definition, I was a paid professional singer before I attended primary school,' she laughs.

'However, the first time I really sang semi-professionally was with the Kingston All Star Showband; I was only fourteen and a pupil at St Mary's in Creggan. How it came about was Gerry O'Neill came to our house to see if our Helen would join his band. But my father told him Helen was living in England. On hearing their conversation, I simply poked my head around the door and said: "I can sing!" Gerry asked my father if he'd let me join the band and he agreed, as he had known Gerry for many years and knew he would look after me. I sang with them for a few months.

'I left St Mary's and started work in Leinster's Shirt Factory before moving on to Tillies. Although putting in a hard day's work in the factories, I still sang at nights. At sixteen, I did a few gigs with the Sky Rockets Showband from Belfast and at seventeen, I was very proud to have won the contralto solo in the Derry Feis.'

When asked if she'd danced much herself, her eyes lit up and she went on to say: 'I loved dancing and the Corinthian Ballroom and Borderland were my favourite dance halls. But my difficulty regarding going dancing was twofold: my friends and dancing pals Molly Harkin from Rossville Street, Una McShane, Josie Coyle and Shelia Bryson were all going steady, and with my singing career now taking off, my dancing days were curtailed somewhat at an early age. It was now a case of me entertaining from the stage rather than being entertained on the dance floor.

'After touring all over Ireland I was advised to move to London, so I left Derry when I was twenty-two. Later, I moved on to Leeds, Manchester and Nottingham, joining the big-band circuit, before heading to America. After a few months in the States, I returned to Derry.

'Back home, I received a telegram from an agent in Glasgow offering me a job. Once again, I got itchy feet, packed my bags and off I went to Scotland. However, when I arrived in Glasgow I discovered no such job existed. I was now in a bit of a pickle: there I was, standing in the middle of Glasgow with no work. I decided straightaway that rather than return to Derry I would look for a job. So in I went to Tiffany's – Scotland's biggest dance-hall chain – to seek employment. As my dear mother used to say, as one door closes, another one opens; and she was definitely correct about that.

'While waiting for the manager, I heard the sound of music coming from the main hall. Being curious, I ventured inside to have a look and I saw this big band practising on stage. As I was about to walk away, I heard someone call my name. Turning around, I saw one of the musicians jump from the stage and run towards me. As he got closer, I recognised him as the piano player from a band I had performed with in London. He threw his arms around me and told me he was delighted to see me. They had a girl singer they were not happy with so they offered me a job in the band right there and then. I gladly accepted and I sang with them for several years.

'Actually, it was while singing with them that I met my husband, Alasdair. He was friendly with our band leader who had introduced me to him one night. After, we had just parted and that was that.

'However, one night after a show, my friend and I were going to a party in Glasgow but we couldn't get a taxi outside Tiffany's. We were standing outside the front door for ages waiting on one. As luck would have it, the next man to appear out of Tiffany's was Alasdair. I went over and asked him for a lift and he said okay, as he was going to the same party. After the party, he asked if he could leave me home and I agreed. He completely swept me off my feet. He was such a lovely man, a compassionate human being and the love of my life. Four short months later, he walked me down the aisle of St Aloysius Chapel in Glasgow and I became Mrs Majella McClimont.

'It was the best contract I have ever signed.

'Sadly, Alasdair passed away three years ago, but we had thirty-three wonderful, happy years living in Edinburgh. Although I still live and have many great friends there, in my mind and heart, Derry will always be home to me. As the old saying goes, you can take the girl out of Derry but not Derry out of the girl.'

When asked if she had any regrets about her career, she replied, 'No, no regrets.' When pushed on this, she said, 'Well, maybe sometimes, just sometimes, I get the feeling I am the forgotten Derry singer.'

After nearly three hours in this charismatic lady's company, I think I can assure her that no-one in Derry forgets Majella Brady or the contribution she's made to the entertainment of the Derry public.

Majella Brady doing what she does best,
singing to a full house at the Embassy in 1968.

Workmates and Dancing Pals

Isabel Doherty remembers the night well. 'It was Saturday 15 April 1961. My friend Dolores Dillon and I were at a dance in the Guildhall. We were standing in our normal spot at the side of the hall when these two young fellows asked us out to dance. I got on well with my fellow; he seemed nice and friendly. When the dance was over, he asked me to keep him another one later on. Some time later, he came back and took me out to dance again, but this time he also asked to leave me home at the end of the night. To be honest, I didn't know what to say, but I agreed to meet him at the bottom of the stairs when the dance was over. However, the very next dance, things took a turn which caused me to change my mind. This time, I was on the floor dancing my feet off with a fellow who seemed to tick all the right boxes for me: he was polite, well dressed and easy to talk to – and not bad-looking either.

David Doherty and Isabel Doherty on their wedding day, 28 January 1964.

'During the set, I found out his name was David Doherty, same surname as me, and that he lived in the Waterside. He invited me to stay on the floor with him for the next dance and it was then he asked if he could walk me to my home in Stanley's Walk. Like a flash, I agreed, but then I remembered about the other young man who would be waiting downstairs for me. My mind was already made up, so there was nothing I could really do about the situation I found myself in. So with eyes fixed straight ahead, and not even throwing him a sideways glance, I walked past him, my arm linked on to David.

'He walked me home that night and we stopped by the gasyard wall for a court. Every time I hear Seán Coyle playing *Dirty Old Town*, I just smile and let my mind slip back to that very first night when David left me home. Actually, on that first date we didn't arrange another one, so we just left it at that. The following Sunday night, I was up the town with my friends and we were walking along Ferryquay Street when I saw David and his mate coming towards us. We stopped and exchanged some small talk, during which my friend Dolores suggested I should ask him to go to the City Factory dance the following week. So I did just that and he readily agreed. In fact, he was chuffed to bits, as he had a grin on his face as wide as the Foyle. Even though we were both only seventeen years old at the time, that was the end of single life for both of us, and we have been together ever since. So what started with that very first kiss by the gasyard wall has stood the test of time. After almost fifty years with him, I think I am entitled to say I made the right choice,' she laughed, looking at David.

David joined the conversation. 'We danced everywhere and saw all the top showbands there was to see. The Derry bands were fantastic and we loved Dickie McManus and the Woodchoppers. Then the big glitzy showmen of the southern showbands came on the scene. It was a time when the dance halls and the picture houses were the only shows in town. But hey, what a time to be young! Our memories of those showband and dance-hall days are just as vivid today as they were all those years ago.'

As David was emphasising to me how good the Lakewood Swingtette were, the doorbell rang. Isabel opened the door and the noise levels rose significantly as Mary Clifford and Clare Bridge, two of Isabel's friends, joined us. With the three old friends now chatting like a runaway train, David, eyebrows raised, quietly made his exit and left them to it.

Clare took centre stage as she reminisced about their antics as young teenage girls doing the dance-hall circuit together. 'We loved the Pallidrome in Strabane

The City Factory, pictured here in the 1930s, employed hundreds of Derry women over the decades.

and would hitchhike a lift from Derry most times. We got a lift one night from Brian Poole and the Tremeloes who were playing there. They took us back stage and even gave us a lift back to Derry after the dance.

However, it was in Borderland that I met Ronnie Moore, who was to become my best friend and the love of my life. It was St Patrick's night 1966 when I first set eyes on him. I noticed him out dancing and he looked strikingly handsome. I was all lured when he came over and asked me out to dance. I remember thinking to myself as we danced, I hope he asks to leave me home. As we danced cheek-to-cheek I noticed he smelt really lovely. But I was always a sucker for the aroma of Old Spice.'

The three friends went into a fit of laughter at this. Clare continues her story.

'Anyway, he asked to leave me

Mary Clifford, Danny Doherty, Clare Bridge and Ronnie Moore at the Embassy in 1965.

home and like a shot, I said okay, why not? I really got excited when he told me he had a car and would give a lift to my friends Mary Clifford and Vera Sheerin. Ronnie was a breadman and at weekends I would accompany him on his round. He was a very caring fellow and had a great zest for life, albeit a little impulsive at times. He was a pilot.'

I looked at her with a puzzled grin and reminded her she had told me he was a breadman. All three broke into loud laughter again.

Clare replied, 'Yes he was, but he also had a pilot's licence for flying light aircraft near where he lived in Eglinton. It was his passion.'

A serious look came over her face then as she told me about their wedding day.

'Ronnie was a Protestant and I was a Catholic, so it was a mixed marriage. Ronnie didn't tell anyone we were getting married, not even his family. That was the way it was back then. Stupid, I know, but that was life in those days. We arranged to meet in a bar on the morning of our wedding; from there we journeyed on to Moville and we got married. That was in December of 1967; Mary was bridesmaid and her husband Danny was best man. Ronnie actually left his home in his working coat on our wedding day so as not to alert anyone. We stayed that night in my mother's house. Ronnie told his family of our wedding two days later. We then went to live in a mobile home near Ballykelly and were deliriously happy in our humble surroundings.

'We had a long and happy life until his untimely death in 2004. I have nothing but the fondest of memories of travelling around to the different dance halls in his wee Clubman Mini estate car. Ah! What would I give now for one more dance at Borderland?' asked Clare.

After a few moments of silence reflecting on what Clare had said, Mary Clifford begins reminiscing about her teenage years. 'I would start getting ready for a dance in my house but would finish getting ready in Clare's house. The reason for this was Clare had all the best make-up. She had everything a chemist shop had to offer, so I took advantage of that. She had Panstick foundation, Pagan and White Fire perfume, Love Affair hairspray and even Miners Lacquer. As far as getting new clothes, we used to get everything on tick. I got mine in Kitty Maguire's wee sweetie shop in Rossville Street. Kitty would give us a ticket to take to Paul's Fashions or Etam. There we could get the modern clothes of our choice to the value on the ticket. We would then pay Kitty a weekly amount. Actually, there was a saying among the factory girls that Etam stood for "Everything To Attract Men".

'We were a very adaptable lot in our factory. For instance, if we couldn't afford curlers to wave our hair, we just used bobbins from the spools of thread.

'I met my husband Danny at the Plaza in Buncrana. I was going out with a Strabane fellow but fell out with him after we had a tiff. So that night, I went with Danny but told him about the Strabane fellow. Still, Danny asked if he could see me the following Tuesday. I told him I would have to contact the Strabane fellow and meet him again for a chat. Danny wasn't keen on that idea, but it was the decent thing to do, so I did just that. I met the Strabane fellow and had a long chat with him. It was during that chat that I knew he wasn't the man for me, so as gently as I could, I finished with him for good.

'The following week I saw Danny at the Plaza again, but he didn't see me, so I just enjoyed the dance. When I boarded the bus for Derry afterwards it was packed. I just stood there on the aisle and grabbed the handrail, expecting a bumpy ride home. Then I heard a voice shouting my name and it was Danny who invited me to sit on his knee. So I planted myself on his lap and we got talking. When we arrived in Derry he walked me home. We made a date for the next night and that was that. A couple of years later we were married.

'Danny died a few years ago, but we had a great life together. Those were brilliant days and they left us with so many happy memories. I still meet up with my old friends to this day, friends I went with to all those dances, and we enjoy reminiscing about old times over a cup of tea.'

Jackie McCauley and Maureen Hazlett at the Cameo in 1965.

Pretty Brown Eyes

'Hey, brown eyes, where do the Dohertys live?' Maureen Hazlett remembers those were the very first words that her husband Jackie McCauley uttered to her, way back in 1964.

'I was in Rinmore Drive talking to my friend Margaret Doherty when Jackie approached and asked me where the Doherty family lived. "Well, you can take your pick, because there are about five Dohertys in this street," I told him.

'"Doherty the window cleaners," he said. So I pointed him in the right direction. The following week I went to the Corinthian and I saw him standing with his hands in his pockets at the back of the hall. When he spotted me, he came over and asked me out to dance. I asked him if he did much dancing, as it was obvious to me he didn't. "Not really. I only know a few steps that my mother taught me," he replied with a smile. I could do nothing but laugh.

'He walked me home that night and my mother liked him the first time she laid eyes on him. She kept saying to me, "You should go out with that wee fellow on a permanent basis. He seems very nice." I told her I thought he was too small. "Love, you don't measure a man by how tall he is," my mother sharply answered back. She was impressed by the fact he sported a pioneer pin on his lapel. I remember her saying to me, "Not too many wee boys have that pin on their coat these days, and mark my words, wee girl, you will be sorry if you let him slip through your fingers."

'Jackie definitely made a good impression on my mother, that's for sure.' Maureen goes in to a fit of giggling when she recalls her granny needed further proof that Jackie was indeed the right boy for her. Maureen wipes away tears of laughter as she goes on to tell me: 'Jackie was standing in our living room with his hands in his pockets as usual. I secretly observed my granny staring at him. Then out of the blue, she said to him, "Walk up and down there, son, so I can get a good look at you."

'For a fleeting moment Jackie was stuck for words. Then he looked at her and said, "What do you think I am, a prize bull?" Honest to God, it was like a scene out of *Hancock's Half-Hour*.

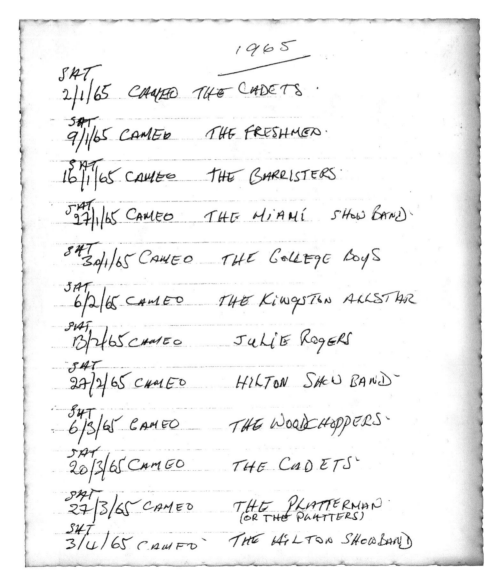

An extract from Maureen Hazlett's 1965 diary.

'I then started going out with him steady and I danced his feet off at all the venues at least three times a week. We had the time of our life seeing all the top showbands – and in every hall in Derry. I kept a diary of all the places we went to and the showbands that were playing.'

To emphasise to me how much dancing they did, Maureen handed me her diary so I could read the entries she'd written. As I took a closer look at this A4-size book, I must admit I was spellbound. Here in my hands was a daily account of her young life and in minute detail. Every dance she attended before and after she met Jackie was recorded here. Plus, every other occasion was noted, no matter how small, and on a daily basis. For instance, one such entry read, 'Jackie was up tonight and I made him soup. He had to leave early.' After discussing some more of the entries in her comprehensive and neatly written diary, Maureen continued her story.

'About a year later, Jackie asked me to get engaged and I told him that would be lovely, but he would have to ask my father's permission.'

Jackie takes up the story.

'It was the norm back then if you were getting engaged to ask for the father's permission. So this night, I asked Joe, Maureen's father. I just said: "I want to get engaged to Maureen, is that okay?" Joe was happy for us and said, "Yes, I have no objections to that as long as you don't rush in to anything too quickly. You both are still very young." So with everyone's blessing, we got engaged in 1965 and were married on Saturday 24 June 1967 in St Mary's Church in Creggan.

Maureen and Jackie cut the cake on their wedding day, Saturday 24 June 1967.

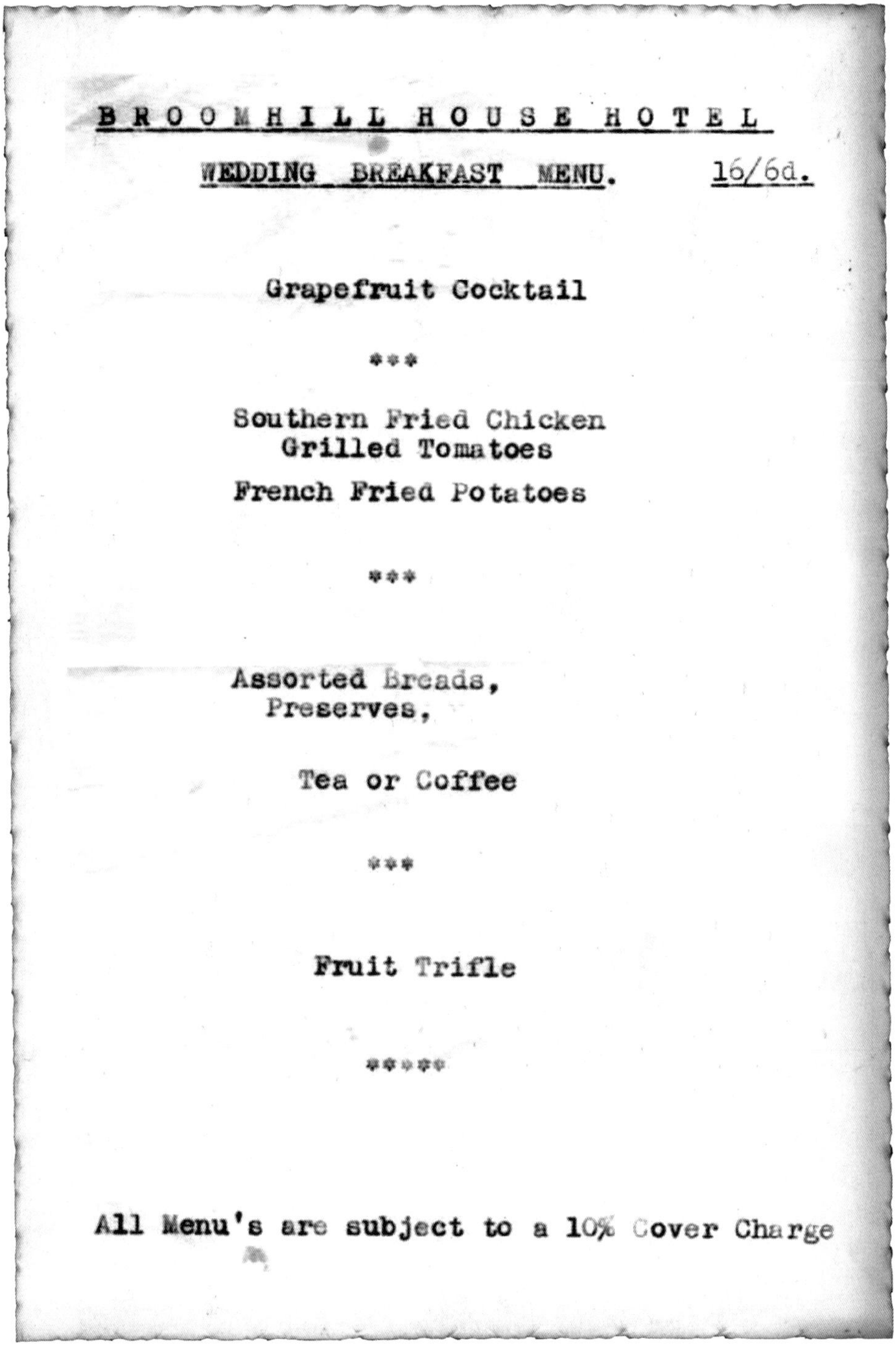

B R O O M H I L L   H O U S E   H O T E L

WEDDING BREAKFAST MENU.   16/6d.

Grapefruit Cocktail

***

Southern Fried Chicken
Grilled Tomatoes
French Fried Potatoes

***

Assorted Breads,
Preserves,

Tea or Coffee

***

Fruit Trifle

****

All Menu's are subject to a 10% Cover Charge

The wedding reception menu for Jackie McCauley and Maureen Hazlett in the Broomhill Hotel in 1967.

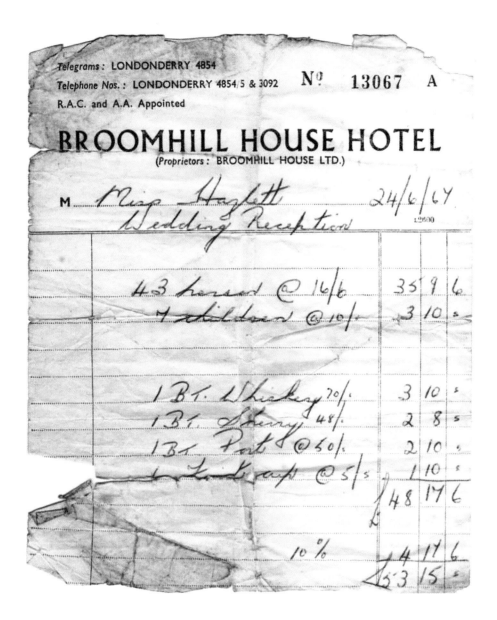

BROOMHILL HOUSE HOTEL
(Proprietors : BROOMHILL HOUSE LTD.)

M .... Miss Hazlett   24/6/64

Wedding Reception   L2600

43 heads @ 16/6	35	9	6
7 children @ 10/-	3	10	=
1 BT. Whiskey 70/-	3	10	=
1 BT. Sherry 48/-	2	8	5
1 BT. Port @ 50/-	2	10	=
...... @ 5/-	1	10	5
	£48	17	6
10%	£4	17	6
	£53	15	=

The bill for Jackie and Maureen's wedding reception.

'Actually, Barry 'Bassy' Mallett and Mary Tierney were married the same day in the same chapel. Our wedding day went brilliantly and we had a great time.'

Jackie's tone of voice changed as he went on to say: 'I had a little scare that night. We were going to the Isle of Man for our honeymoon and as we were flying out of Aldergrove Airport the following day, we decided to stay the night in Hall's Hotel in Antrim.

133

'We settled in to our hotel, but later that night Maureen asked me to go to the shop nearby for some chocolate. I rushed to the shop before it closed, but when I got back to the hotel the front door was locked. I knocked loudly to attract the night porter's attention and after about ten minutes he came to the door. At first he wouldn't believe I was a guest at the hotel, but after about five minutes arguing with him, I persuaded him to check the register. After what seemed an eternity, he finally let me in.

'That incident scared the life out of me, because for those few minutes, I had visions of me spending my wedding night on the street.'

Maureen, laughing heartily, went on to say, 'When Jackie came in to our hotel room, he told me what had happened. I was sitting on the bed with the sheets folded back neatly and wearing a peach negligee. Jackie, with a smile on his face, went into the bathroom to get ready for bed. And, God love him, he still must have been in shock because he appeared from the bathroom wearing a pair of green and white striped pyjamas. He looked like a scallion,' roared Maureen with laughter.

Brian Heaney and Ann Brown smooching around the Stardust in 1966. In the background is John Smith.

Maureen continued: 'In the Isle of Man we spent everything we had and we arrived back in Derry with ten bob between us. We got a taxi to our wee flat at 42 Beechwood Avenue and we were blissfully happy living there until we got a house in Creggan. Brian Heaney and his new bride Ann Brown were living in the other flat in the same building. We struck up a great friendship with them while living there and we still socialise together to this day.'

I met up with Brian Heaney, whom I've known from my school days, and he went on to tell me how he met his wife Ann.

'Ann was a friend of my sister Rosemary, as they both worked in the same shirt factory. My sister told our family that a workmate was coming out to our house to visit her this night. Well, that workmate just happened to be Ann and that was the first time I saw her. I must admit I fancied her from the word go and fate threw us together. Soon, Ann was coming out to our wee home at Sandbank Cottages, not to see my sister but to see me,' laughs Brian. 'I offered to take her to a dance and she agreed and we enjoyed each other's company so much we decided to make the arrangement permanent,' he says with a smile.

Ann Brown and Brian Heaney are in happy spirits at the Stardust in 1966 as Dinny McGinley looks on in the background.

First Dance and a Blind Date

It was the trend in the 1960s for the girls to go to the dances at a younger age than the boys. This was probably because their make-up and style of dress made them look much older whereas the fifteen- or sixteen-year-old boys still looked their age or even younger. It was then the custom for the younger ones to go to the small 'hops' where only records were played until they graduated to the 'big' dances.

Helen Anderson.

Helen Duffy (née Anderson) from the Lecky Road remembers her first big dance well. 'God, even though it was over forty-five years ago, I can remember every minute of it. The lead-up to it was hell: sleepless nights, the loss of appetite, concentration gone completely askew.

'It was a Friday and although I was at school, to tell you the truth I was so excited I never heard a word any of the teachers said that day.' Helen clasps a cup of tea in her hands as she laughs and continues her account of that memorable occasion. 'After coming through the gates of St Mary's School, I walked as fast as I could down to my Lecky Road home. As I entered our wee terraced house, I threw my schoolbag on our sofa and my mother told me my tea was ready in the scullery.

'Out I went and nibbled at my tea and when I convinced my mother I had eaten enough, it was off to the bedroom to prepare for the biggest night of my young life. Not that I had to make any big decision on what to wear, mind you, as I only had the one good dress and one good pair of shoes.

'The four hours or so to the bus time dragged so slowly as I sat on my bed and looked into the mirror perched on top of our chest of drawers. I thought to myself, I can't believe I will see him in person on stage. I mean, I will only be a few feet away from Dickie Rock. My heart was pounding. Eventually, the time had come for us to leave and walk the short distance to Patrick Street to catch the bus to Muff. Crossing William Street, I asked Stella McBrearty what I should do if a fellow asked me to dance, what should I say? "Just keep your mouth shut and start dancing," she giggled back.

'As the bus pulled out of Patrick Street, I was feeling nervous and thinking, what if the bouncers don't let us in because we are too young. But I was fairly sure we would be okay because I knew some of the boys working the door that night.

Borderland advertising from 1959 and 1969.

'On entering Borderland, my first impression was it looked so big, but when the pubs closed and the men started filing in, it was soon packed. We had an absolute ball and when the night was over we couldn't wait to go back again.'

Helen's husband John entered the living room. I nodded towards him and asked Helen how and where they met. 'Now, that's another story,' she said, smiling as she glanced at John.

'It was actually a blind date. Stella McBrearty was taking John McDaid, from the Waterside, to a dinner dance and she asked him to bring a friend to accompany me. He brought John. After the dance was over, the two boys said, "Well, since you took us out tonight, we will return the favour and take you both out next weekend." We agreed.

'The next weekend we went to the pictures and John asked me to go to the Stardust with him the following night, which I did. From there on we started to see each other pretty often and soon we were going out steady.

'John started to play football for Derry City and after training he would walk over the Lecky Road to see me before going to his home in the Waterside. As John was playing every Saturday we didn't get to Borderland much on a Friday night. So we nearly always went to the Stardust, which John liked the best anyway, or the Embassy. We did, however, get to Borderland on some Friday nights when the football season was over.

'We got engaged the following year and that was another story, God knows,' she said, eyebrows raised. I looked at Helen and asked her to keep on talking.

John Duffy and Helen Anderson on their wedding day. At the car window is a young fan, probably looking for John's autograph. John was, of course, the star player in the Derry City team at the time.

'Well, normally people get engaged when out for a meal, at a party or even out on a walk on a summer's night – you know, something a wee bit romantic. But where did we get engaged?' she asked, arms outstretched. 'We got engaged on the roadside in the middle of nowhere. It was Thursday 3 October 1968 and we were going to a party in Keady, Armagh, which was being held by John's family to celebrate his twenty-first birthday.

'The car in which we were travelling broke down on a country road and we were standing on the roadside. Freddie Blakeley was tampering with the engine in an effort to get it running again. I turned to John and said, "Some night this is going to be." He smiled back at me and whispered, "It might be a better night than you think." Then he put his hand in his pocket and pulled out this lovely small box. He opened it and there was a beautiful, sparkling engagement ring. There and then he asked me if I wanted to get engaged. I was flabbergasted. "Yes I would," I said in a flash. He slipped the ring onto my finger, kissed me and said we were now officially engaged. I was speechless and I just looked at him. The next thing I heard was Freddie shouting to us, "Let's give this car a push now and try and get it started."

'So I started life as an engaged girl by pushing an old banger down a country road in the middle of County Armagh. But to tell you the truth, I was feeling so good at that particular moment that I could have pushed a double-decker bus up Southway.

'In July 1970, he walked me down the aisle in the Long Tower Church. That was forty years ago and we now have five children and eight grandchildren. And he is still as romantic today as ever he was.'

A view of the very impressive Embassy Ballroom, arguably one of the best laid out and maintained dance halls in the country.

The Embassy Ballroom

Even though the promoters and ballroom owners around the country were pocketing great profits, most still refused to invest any of it in making the ballrooms more comfortable for their patrons. To be quite frank, some of the rural 'ballrooms' were nothing more than large barns with four walls and a tin roof, with no dressing-room facilities for the bands or any real comfort for the dancers. The car-parking facilities were mere fields of rough ground with gravel thrown over them.

The dance halls in the cities tended to be of a better quality with Derry's Embassy Ballroom being probably the most luxurious. The hallway and stairs leading to the ballroom were always kept clean and brightly lit. It had plush carpets throughout and the dance floor itself was always highly polished. The balcony had modern chairs and tables, and the toilets were always spotless. Patrons could sit and have a mineral and watch the dancers below or just listen to the band in great comfort.

It would also be fair to say the Embassy had a far more progressive management team than most ballrooms. It was owned by Tony Kearney, a gentleman who deserved more credit than maybe he got. His contribution to the entertainment of the dancers in Derry was immense. Tony provided a safe, friendly and comfortable atmosphere where everyone could enjoy a night of great dancing. The management team responsible for the day-to-day running of the Embassy was led by popular local businessman Robert (Bobby) Ferris. It was obvious Bobby had his finger on the pulse, as his team were very clued in to what made the young people tick. They

Tony Kearney, proprietor of the Embassy Ballroom, having a quiet drink with former Miss Ireland, Susanna Riddell.

always provided top-class entertainment and audiences were able to enjoy international star performers there several times a year.

Competitions which caught the imagination of the young dancers were held at regular intervals: these included the Smartest Girl in Town, Miss Teen Derry, Miss Embassy and local heats of Miss Ireland for the ladies, while the Dandy Debonair or Mr Poser for the young men would create a bit of light relief and banter for all concerned. Dandy Debonair was for the best-dressed man and Mr Poser was for the biggest show-off in the hall who fancied himself as a ladies man. Some men would come dressed to the nines, with new suit, matching tie and handkerchief in the breast pocket, hair cut to perfection with just the right amount of Brylcreem on and soaked in Old Spice aftershave.

Naturally, the men tried their best to pretend they were not interested in attracting the attention of the judges, who usually were some well-known local ladies. Nevertheless, when they did manage to do just that they had a grin on their face as wide as the Foyle. As for the ladies' competitions, I can say with a fair degree of certainty that they most definitely did take their contests very seriously indeed. As did some of their mothers who normally would observe proceedings from the comfort of the balcony.

One thing I think most people would agree on was that the prettiest girls were usually standing on the floor looking up at the stage. That is not to say the girls on stage were not pretty; of course they were. But if you had asked anyone to pick out the prettiest girl in the hall, I would have been fairly confident the winner would have come from the floor.

These young ladies are hoping to catch the judges' eye in the 1970 Miss Derry competition in the Embassy. Front: Lily Hanlon, Margaret Hogan and Eilish McCafferty. Back: Hazel Caldwell and Philomena Doherty.

Four lovely ladies at the Embassy in 1968: Angela Fleming, Jennifer Devlin, Sally McCauley and Katherine Golden.

It is also fair comment to say the competitions brought a mixed reaction from some of the male dancers. Some simply disliked them and couldn't wait to get them over. Then they could get back to the serious business of dancing and trying to meet a woman while others enjoyed the craic and banter. And everyone had an opinion afterwards. This was exactly the outcome the organisers had hoped for. What is certain is that Robert Ferris afforded the young women who danced in the Embassy an opportunity to carve out a career in modelling – or even show business – through such competitions. He also afforded the same opportunity to some of the young men, as he brought John O'Driscoll, Pat McAllister and Bo O'Donnell to prominence as disc jockeys.

Arguably one of the most popular bands to play the Embassy was the Chessmen, who had a massive following. Popular local man Gerry Anderson played lead guitar with them. They were one of the new emerging 'pop' showbands and when they were in the Embassy, you couldn't get moving in it. Their performances were always eagerly awaited by the young dancers, as they put on a non-stop, upbeat show, which the young teenagers loved.

I remember well the night the top English band, Dave Dee, Dozy, Beaky, Mick and Titch came to play the Embassy. There was a large crowd outside the venue and excitement was running high, as everyone wanted to catch a glimpse of this famous group. When they eventually arrived, they ran so fast into the building, all you could see were their long fur coats flying past you.

The most famous DJ of all time, Jimmy Saville, was another big name to play there. Bobby Ferris remarked: 'Jimmy Saville came across as a nice, down-to-earth gentleman and lovely to work with. He made a great impression with our young patrons and enhanced his reputation no end as far as the teenagers of Derry were concerned. Engelbert Humperdinck was also to grace the Embassy stage and he too was a gentleman and easy to work with.'

The dancers of Derry were entertained by numerous international stars at the Embassy, stars they would never have seen but for Ferris and Kearney. Both men made a significant contribution to establishing the Embassy Ballroom as one of the best-kept and best-run venues in the country. Bobby was a very popular man with the dancers, as he was always keen to listen to their opinions. A well-known Embassy patron remarked: 'As far as the entertainment of the youth of this city was concerned, Bobby Ferris was a man before his time. As a teenager, I saw big stars I would never have seen, thanks to him.'

Lulu 'shouts' at the Embassy Ballroom, c.1967.

Above: Selected for Heat 1 of Miss Teen Derry 1968 are, at back, Philomena Sheerin, Angela Fleming, Doris McMenamin and Pat O'Connell. Seated are Bernadette Lynch and Veronica Carlin. Below: Heat 2. Included are Linda McNulty, Mary Lou Moore, Emer O'Brien, Maureen Brown, Rosemary Thompson and Ann Reilly.

Above: Heat 3. Mary Frazer, Marie O'Kane, Jacqueline Hutchinson, Veronica McDaid and, seated, Bridgeen Carr. Below: Heat 4. Back: Kathleen Donaghey, Margaret McLaughlin, Kay Nash, Isa Doherty and Kathleen Stewart. Seated: Judges Joan McGinty and Mary McGinty of SHE Boutique.

Above: Heat 5. Philomena Boyle, Ann Harkin, Donna McDonnell, Lucy McConway and Kerona Glenn. Below: Heat 6. Olive Murray, Madeleine McGonagle, Rosemary Doherty and Kathy Ramsey. Seated: Una Harkin and Kathleen Quigley.

Right: Heat 7. Margaret Crumley, Geraldine Mullan and Olive Sheerin.

Below: Heat 8. Back: Majella Crawley, Isa Moore and Cecilia Milne. Seated: Daphne Doherty and Margaret McCallion.

Above: The final of Miss Teen Derry 1968 held in the Embassy Ballroom.
Manager Robert Ferris with judges Majella Brady, Martin Lewis and JB Glover. Seated
are Kathy Ramsey, who came second, Isa Moore, the winner, and in third place, Kerona
Glenn. Below: The Embassy Ballroom in the 1960s.

Former Romper Room *children's TV presenter Helen Madden (left) and Robert Ferris, the Embassy manager, present a bouquet to Miss Teen Ireland Majella Crawley, c.1967.*

Enjoying another night out at the Embassy in 1967 are Majella Crawley, Barbara McClintock and June Armstrong.

A crowded Embassy dance floor in 1971. Looking happy as he danced is Don McAnaney on the extreme right.

Coyle and Co. Six young lads taking their dose of Dutch courage before going on to the Embassy in 1968. Included are Gabriel Bell, Liam Gallagher, Seán Coyle, Eunan Deeney, James Kelly and John Houston. Captured at the Hayloft Bar, where the young men were enjoying the music of Jim 'Fingers' Bradley and Frankie Robinson.

No Strings Attached

BBC Radio Foyle's Seán Coyle freely admits the Embassy was one of his favourite dance halls and during our conversation several events sprang to mind on which he reminisced. One was the occasion he met his wife Patricia and the unusual circumstances in which their first date came about. Another was at the ripe old age of seventeen when he made his first trip to England.

Seán explains: 'I was seventeen, unemployed and with a chip on my shoulder – I wanted to change the world. I set off on my first trip to Birmingham in England. With suitcase in hand, I left our wee terraced home and made my way to the Waterside station. There, I boarded a train which was to take me somewhere near the airport where my plane bound for Birmingham was waiting. It was there I was to make my fortune, but if truth be told, all I ever wanted were new clothes and the fare home! I stayed there for nearly a year and worked on the building sites where one of my workmates was Engelbert Humperdinck. England was okay, but I was hankering for the Derry dance halls, the showbands and my mates.

'I gathered enough money to buy the latest gear, the fare home and to put a few pounds in my Post Office savings book. That's all I needed; that's all I ever wanted. So I booked my flight home, my objectives achieved. That was the end of my travels away from home.'

Seán then told of how he met his wife Patricia.

'It came about really on the day I offered to baby-sit for Victor Walker and his wife. Normally, baby-sitting wouldn't have been a problem, but on this particular

152

night, it was. I had just finished with my girlfriend and now found myself in a bit of a jam. I mean, I couldn't appear at Victor's door on my own to baby-sit; it just wasn't the done thing. It was taken that you would have a girl with you. So I had to put my thinking cap on. At that time, my mates and I were friendly with a group of girls we always danced with in the Embassy. Both of our groups had one thing in common: we liked the Beach Boys' hit *Help Me, Rhonda*.

'Among that group was Patricia. I tentatively approached her and told her my situation and I asked her if she'd baby-sit with me, with no strings attached. She agreed to help me out of the predicament I found myself in. The baby-sitting duties went smoothly and at the end of the evening, I really wanted to ask her out on a proper date. But as I had told her there were no strings attached, I didn't know what her reaction would be.

'As I walked her home, I kept tossing it about in my head, but I really wanted to ask her out. So I just took the bull by the horns and asked her if she'd fancy going to the pictures some night. I was chuffed when she said yes, so two nights later we went to the pictures. That date led to other dates and soon we were going steady. As a couple, we went to every dance hall around, danced to every showband in sight and went to every picture house in Derry.

'Now, every time I hear the Beach Boys singing *Help Me, Rhonda*, I think of the Embassy Ballroom. And every time I walk past the old Embassy building, I stop and look up at it and say to myself, one night I walked through those doors and before the night was over, I had met my wife.'

One of Seán's other favourite dance halls was the Plaza Ballroom in Buncrana.

'The Plaza dance floor was fantastic; it just had a natural spring. It was the best I ever danced on.'

Seán reckons it was a close call between all the dance halls he and Patricia had visited as to which was his favourite.

'They were all great halls. Can I hedge my bets and say Borderland and the Plaza in Donegal, and the Embassy in Derry? All had their own unique qualities, atmosphere and crowds.'

He laughs as he recalled one particular incident which caused him some slight embarrassment.

'Every time I hear Larry Cunningham singing, I think back to this one night in particular. I was at the Plaza and boy, did I put my foot in it. I missed the bus home, as did three other Derry people, John Houston, Margaret Bell and Theresa McCallion. There was nothing we could do but start the long walk from Buncrana back to Derry.

'The band on stage that night was Larry Cunningham and the Mighty Avons. Although they had a massive Irish hit with *Among The Wicklow Hills*, they were not to my liking. It wasn't that they were not a good band, it was because they played country music, and each song sounded the same to me. The drummer played the same beat to all the songs that night.'

Jim 'Fingers' Bradley and Majella Brady after a gig at the old City Hotel in 1965.

Right: Derry City footballer Joe Nicholl enjoying a dance at the Plaza with his girlfriend Bridget Fletcher in August 1968.

Joe Nicholl and his new bride on their wedding day with bridesmaid Kathleen Fletcher and best man Jamesie Nicholl.

A typical night in the Embassy Ballroom. The girls on the left are waiting to be 'lifted' but the shy men on the right are not for moving.

The best front men of the best bands: Joe Dolan, Art Supple, Dickie Rock, Tom Dunphy, Brendan Bowyer, Derek Dean, Brendan O'Brien, Butch Moore, Larry Cunningham, Declan Ryan and Tony Kneeling.

Seán breaks in to song as he sings *Simple Simon Says* in a country beat, just to give me an idea what he meant about the Mighty Avons' drummer. I could do nothing but laugh.

Seán continues: 'As the four of us were walking along the Buncrana to Derry road, a minibus pulled up and offered us a lift to Derry. We got in and began chatting to the lads in the bus. One of them asked me where we were that night and I told him we were at the Plaza. Another enquired if I'd enjoyed my night there. I told him not really, the band wasn't very good, they were a country band and they sang every song to the same beat. After a few moments of silence, I asked them where they were they had been. "Ah, we were the band playing in the Plaza," replied one of them. I nearly fainted and Derry couldn't come quickly enough for the four of us that night. I still shudder to this day when that incident comes to mind. But the boys in the van just laughed it off and were quite nice about it really.'

Seán's view of country music would have been the opinion held by the vast majority of Derry dance-goers, including Yours Truly, who simply disliked it. Country bands, even to this day, do not enjoy great popularity in Derry.

I remember a conversation Fr Brian Darcy had once on his BBC Radio Ulster show with arguably Ireland's best country singer of the showband era, Brian Coll from Omagh. Part of the conversation was why country bands got the thumbs down from the Derry and Belfast public. Brian readily agreed that the dance-goers of those cities abhorred country music and that country bands simply just bypassed them on their tours.

Good mates George Lynch, Stevie Wilkinson and Charlie Ferry at the Stardust in 1967.

One showband who had no trouble in attracting crowds in the cities or country dance halls was the Royal Showband. The Royal, formerly known as the Harry Boland Band, was formed in Waterford in 1957. After playing in mainly local halls, they became a big hit with the teenage dancers. Following this initial success, they decided the only way they could improve their prospects further was to buy better equipment that would give them a more powerful sound on stage. They contacted a musical store that offered hire-purchase payment terms and the company sent out their salesman TJ Byrne to meet the band.

After discussing the hire-purchase agreement, Byrne decided to return the next night to hear them playing at a local hall. Byrne looked at the seven young musicians with an average age of eighteen and thought to himself this would be interesting. However, when the band started playing Byrne was flabbergasted, as the whole hall was filled with a tremendous sound and the dancers loved every minute of it. He was suitably impressed and after some discussions with Tom Dunphy, the band's leader, he suggested a further meeting with them to discuss their future.

A week later they met and Byrne emerged as their manager. Following the lead given by Strabane's Clipper Carlton, he immediately changed the band's name to the Royal Showband. Soon they were playing all the top venues in Ireland to sell-out crowds and receiving standing ovations everywhere. They then, along with the Johnny Quigley All Stars and the Clipper Carlton, became one of the top draws in Irish entertainment.

Despite this great success, TJ Byrne was not happy with just conquering the Irish scene; he wanted to do the same with the English market. He secured bookings in mainly Irish dance halls around Britain and just as in Ireland, they went down well everywhere they played. Still, their manager was not fully content, as the biggest

Dickie Rock of the Miami Showband with the Embassy Ballroom's 'Trendsetters' dancers – Gabrielle Perry, Jennifer Monk and Kerona Glenn.

venues in Britain were the world-renowned Mecca ballrooms owned and managed by the impresario Eric Morley.

Byrne tried twice without success to obtain a booking for the Royal from Morley. But Byrne, a Carlow man, was not easily put off, and once again he turned up at Eric Morley's plush office. This third time was definitely lucky as he finally persuaded Morley to give the Irish band a chance, and he obtained a booking at the Hammersmith Palais in London on St Patrick's night in 1960.

The scenes outside the Hammersmith Palais that night were amazing, the queue stretching back hundreds of yards. That night, London's most famous dance venue was to host its biggest-ever crowd.

Just two short months later, the Royal appeared at the Empire Ballroom in Liverpool; once again, the venue was sold out. The support act to the Royal was a local Liverpool group called the Silver Beatles, who would later take Silver out of their name to become – the Beatles. After the dance, a young Paul McCartney and John Lennon were eating fish and chips outside the ballroom and were standing admiring the Royal's new Mercedes van.

Lennon remarked to Brendan Bowyer as the Royal members were getting into their van to leave: 'Well for you, boys.' This was scouse-speak for well done.

Bowyer stopped to talk with both lads and gave them a little bit of advice: 'Boys, you were great tonight and if you stick together you will do well.' Sound advice as the whole world now knows.

Actually, a little known fact is that the Royal Showband was the very first Irish band or artist to record a pop song. They also registered eight consecutive No 1 hits in the Irish hit parade, a feat never since equalled. Of course, as we all know, *The Hucklebuck* was probably the most popular of showband songs and is regarded as the showband anthem.

The band played together for fifteen years without a single change to their line-up before Bowyer left to form his new band, the Big Eight. Later they travelled to Las Vegas where they played for many years and where Bowyer still resides to this day.

*Doc Carroll &
the Royal Blues
Showband.*

According to different polls conducted over the years on Irish radio stations and the internet, the top ten most popular showband songs would be:

1	*The Hucklebuck*	Brendan Bowyer & The Royal
2	*Every Step Of The Way*	Dickie Rock & The Miami
3	*Make Me An Island*	Joe Dolan & The Drifters
4	*My Own Peculiar Way*	Joe Dolan & The Drifters
5	*Walking The Streets In The Rain*	Butch Moore & The Capitol
6	*Black Velvet Band*	Johnny Kelly & The Capitol
7	*Old Man Trouble*	Doc Carroll &The Royal Blues
8	*If I Didn't Have A Dime*	Tom Dunphy & The Royal
9	*Papa Oo Mow Mow*	Derek Dean & The Freshmen
10	*Candy Store*	Dickie Rock & The Miami

The Freshmen

Considered by many to be the best showband of them all, the Freshmen, on stage with Derek Dean at the mike. Also included is the multitalented Billy Brown.

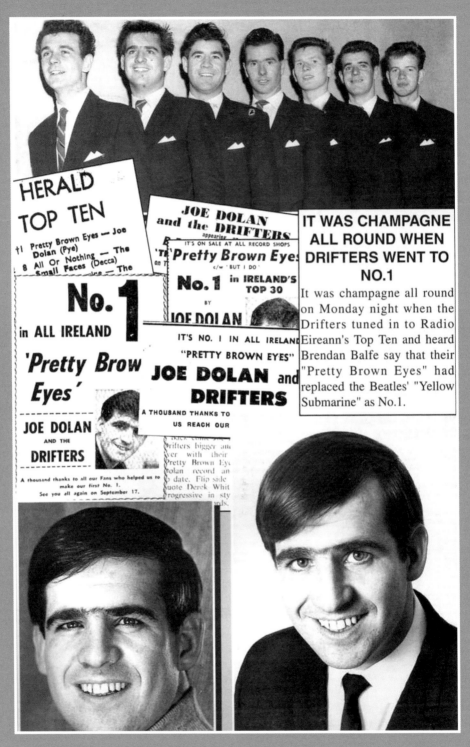

Joe Dolan and the Drifters attracted an amazing 4,200 happy dancers to Borderland in October 1968 – a record for the venue.

The Plaza Ballroom

Buncrana's favourite showband back in the 1960s were undoubtedly the Mighty Rhythm Boys. Not only were they popular in their home town but also throughout Ireland. They started off as the resident band in the Plaza, but their talents were such that they decided to take the plunge and started touring Ireland.

Speaking to Colm Smith, who played piano, it was evident he was very proud of being a founder member of the Mighty Rhythm Boys. Colm, to-day a sprightly eighty-year-old, reminisced about his days travelling to halls in every county.

'They were hard days but very enjoyable and we were lucky to have a great van to travel in. It

Advert for the Plaza in 1969.

had three heaters, which was handy on cold and frosty winter nights. We also fitted the van out with old aeroplane seats, which were very comfortable. The showbands back then were very close and worked together. For example, we would tell bands from Derry about different dance halls and promoters who were looking to book acts and the Derry bands would do the same for us. And several weeks later, as we travelled through the different counties on our way to a gig, we would notice posters nailed to telegraph poles advertising some Derry showbands for those dance halls. We got great satisfaction from that.'

Above: More famous than the beach in Buncrana was Donegal's favourite band, the Mighty Rhythm Boys, plus one lady! Below: A Navy man getting a strange look from a local as he wows a pretty girl at the Plaza Ballroom, Buncrana, in 1965.

Colm said he loved playing in Derry's Guildhall, as the acoustics were fantastic and it was only up the road from Buncrana. The Derry showbands in turn loved playing the Plaza for the same reasons. When asked would he do it all again, his answer was quick and to the point: 'Definitely, but I would ask for more money, because I think, looking back, some of the hall owners were a little too greedy.'

That was a sentiment held by many other showbands of that era.

Buncrana was a favourite spot for many Derry people at the weekends for four main reasons: the beach, football, pubs and the Plaza Ballroom. One Derryman who loved visiting the County Donegal town was John 'Skin' Gillespie. John talks freely of the days of his youth.

'The Lecky Road was the centre of the universe when I was growing

Enjoying a night out at the Plaza in Buncrana, c.1967. John McClean, Pennyburn Church's favourite altar boy, with girlfriend Dolores Hagan from Melmore Gardens on left and Kathleen Coyle, who later married John's friend Charlie Morrison.

up. Everyone passed the Lecky Road on match days at the Brandywell and on their way back they stopped for fish and chips at Maggie Friel's or Harley's. Practically everyone in Derry drank in one of the bars on the Lecky Road or Rossville Street. Everyone brought their rags and porter bottles to Morgan's rag store facing our wee house. Even the great 'Big O' himself, Roy Orbison, walked the Lecky Road to inhale the clean, fresh air before he took to the stage in the Cameo. Enough about the Lecky Road, or Nell might start on about the Camp,' he laughs.

John then talked about his dancing days.

'Ah, the dance hall and showband days, what a time to be young. How could you forget them? Dickie McManus, Gay McIntyre, Johnny Quigley, Mick McWilliams, Johnny Patterson, Don Carlin, stout on sale at 1/3d and five Park Drive for 9d. Then along came the likes of Dickie Rock, Joe Dolan, Brendan Bowyer, Butch Moore, Eileen Reid, the Stones, the Beatles, the list is almost endless.

'They were fantastic days. Packed halls and not a pint to be bought, just jiving the night away with not a penny in your pocket but happy as Larry. Back then, if you passed someone you knew in the street, you would ask them, "Are you going up tonight?" This meant are you going to the Corinthian tonight, that's how popular the Corinthian was.'

e of Derry's many characters, John
ne started his dancing career, like so
ii.. iy others, by going to the hops in St
Mary's and the Wolfe Tone halls. Then it
was on to the big dance halls, the Corinthian, the Crit and the Guildhall.

'I remember the first time I went to
hear a big southern showband; it was in
the Guildhall and Brendan Bowyer and
the Royal were playing. It was ten bob to
get in and I thought it was a bit steep, as
a bottle of stout was only one shilling and
three pence. Everything was measured by
the price of drink back then,' he remarks
with a serious look on his face and eyebrows raised just to emphasise the point.
'But Bowyer and the Royal were something else that night; they were brilliant.
I finished the night soaking in sweat; I
danced my feet off.

'The usual Saturday-night ritual for
Frankie McCauley, Robert Anderson and
me was to get six bottles of stout and five
Woodbine each. The fags were 9d for a
packet of five and the half-dozen of stout
was 7/6d, and the entrance fee for the
dance would normally be a dollar (25p).
Even if we only had a pound each in our
pockets, that left us with enough to buy
a girl a mineral at the dance if we got off,
and a fish supper on the way home.

'If we didn't get off, which in my case
was rarely, then it was straight to Maggie Friel's for a fish supper and a bottle of
lemonade to wash it down. That would
cost about one and a tanner. We could
have a very good night out for a pound
back then.

'I remember going to see Derry play
Glentoran in a cup match in Belfast with
Frankie McCauley and both of us dressed
in Teddy Boy suits. We went over to the

*The quiet man himself, the incomparable
Don Carlin, with girlfriend Celine Ryan
at the Cameo in 1964. Their first date was
at the Emily Ford dance in the Corinthian
on 24 September 1963.*

*Mary Hourigan and John Barr dancing
at Borderland in 1961. On stage singing
is Chuck McGuigan.*

164

The Barristers Showband with Mick Cassidy and Trish Doherty in the mid-'60s.

train station and bought our tickets and there were hundreds of BSR workers at the station all going to support Derry. Frankie and me went over to the Bat and Ball Bar beside the station and bought a dozen bottles of stout. We drank them on the train and after the match, someone told us the Barristers Showband was playing in the Boom Boom Rooms that night. Over we went to the dance, even though we had no money left. I told the bouncers that Mick Cassidy, who was the singer with the Barristers, was my brother and I had to meet him there. The bouncer went inside to verify our story and out came Mick and Chuck McGuigan. Before either could say a word, I winked at Mick and said, "What's the craic, big brother?" All they could do was laugh and they took us in to the dance. We had a ball that night and we got a lift back to Derry with the band. Those were the mad things you did back then, really innocent things like that.

'But some nights things were not so innocent, because there was many a battle royal between the sailors and the local boys. And some local lads got more than they bargained for on occasions, as some of the sailors were no mugs and could handle themselves.'

I inquired if he was ever involved in a scuffle with any of the visiting foreigners. Shaking his head, he said, 'Not really, I was a lover, not a fighter. But I got myself into many a mess, especially with my da, mainly because I came home late, about six in the morning and drunk. I got the odd hand across the back of my head; I was still afraid of my da at that time. The problem with my da was he could hear the grass grow. No front doors were ever locked in those days, just a shoelace on the latch, and all you did was pull the string to open the front door, but he still heard me coming in.

'One mess I got myself into, which I will never forget, was over a coat! We were going to the Plaza in Buncrana and before the dance we were drinking in a bar. We left the bar at 11.00pm and headed across the road to the Plaza. I had a fair amount to drink and the bouncers wouldn't let me in. They told me to take a walk and come back in about twenty minutes. I wasn't very happy about that, as I had a date with a girl and I was supposed to see her inside the hall. A lot of the men did that, as it saved them paying for the girl to get into the dance; money was tight in those days.

'I thought of a way of getting into the Plaza straightaway. As I had no overcoat on at the time, I thought the bouncers wouldn't recognise me with one on. So I went back to the bar and asked Joe Duggan, who was drinking there, for a loan of his overcoat. Joe, who lived beside me, wanted to know why I needed his coat to go to a dance. So I told him the craic and he agreed to loan it to me. It was a brand-new, three-quarter-length overcoat, and he made me promise to leave it back the following morning.

'I put on the coat and over I go again to the front door of the Plaza, but a sharp-eyed bouncer recognised me. He told me to take another walk for five minutes or so and then he would let me in. I turned the corner and walked down towards Maginn Park football pitch. It was very dark and I tripped and fell flat on my face and my blood ended up all over Duggan's new coat.

'By the time I got myself cleaned up and straightened out, the dance was over and Duggan's new overcoat was in a right mess. The next day I had to dodge Duggan, as his coat was

Margaret Herron, Jim Duggan and Maureen Hazlett, three dancing pals on a shopping trip for new clothes to impress in 1965.

Advert from the Derry Journal, *1960.*

Nell Mooney and John 'Skin' Gillespie at a showband dance in the Guildhall in 1963.

only fit for Morgan's rag store, the shape it was in. That morning when the shops opened, I was up like a flash to Lilliput dry-cleaners in the Diamond to get the coat cleaned. But they told me they wouldn't have it done for several days, so that was no good. I then went to Peerless valet dry-cleaners; they, too, couldn't manage it on time. I was now panicking.

'Then I had a brainwave. I went over to the Weaver to Wearer clothes shop in Ferryquay Street, and to my relief, there was the identical coat on a dummy in their window with a price tag on it. I went in and paid a dollar down and signed to pay up weekly for it. I gave Duggan back the new coat; he never knew the difference and I kept his old coat. I had that coat for years after.'

I asked John how and where he met Nell, an old neighbour of mine, and his wife of forty-five years.

'Actually, I had a date with another girl that night and again I was supposed to see her inside the venue. It was a dance over the Collon Lane in the British Legion hall. It was only a husker of a place, but look, if a wee boy was banging on toy drums, I would jive to it. Anyway, the singer in the band announced a ladies' choice and Nell made a beeline for me and asked me to dance. Thankfully, I had the good sense to accept and that was the start of it. We eventually got engaged in 1964 and married the next year.

'Looking back, we had a great time in our youth. We had dancing almost nightly and in the summer we would think nothing of travelling as far as Portrush or Bundoran to see a band.'

John went on to tell me about some embarrassing moments he had during his carefree philandering days.

'I had a couple of false teeth in and I was up in the balcony in the Corinthian. I was hanging over the railing looking to see who was in and they fell out of my mouth and onto the floor below. I flew down the stairs like a rocket and just retrieved them in the nick of time before the next dance started and they got jived on!

'Ah, the craic was mighty when I was a teenager. I often tell my sons that we had more entertainment choices in one night than they have in a month! The youth of today have nothing compared to what we had back then as far as entertainment is concerned. I wouldn't swap it for anything, no chance.

'Just think back: six bottles of stout, a half-bottle of Mundies, five Woodbine and a dance, all for a pound. *Rock Around The Clock*, *The Twist*, *The Hucklebuck*, the Woodchoppers, the Miami, the Freshmen, the Royal, the Rolling Stones, the Beatles, how could you beat that?' he asks, arms outstretched.

John concluded by saying, 'I lived my life to the full as a young man. I had a ball, never caused trouble to anyone, married a good woman, and if I had my life to live over again, I wouldn't change a single day of it.'

Nell Mooney, John 'Skin' Gillespie and friends enjoying a night out in the 1960s.

Not a good idea! But Woodbine were cheap and popular back then.

The People's Champion, John 'Skin' Gillespie, sharing a dance with a friend before the final of the jiving competition at the Stardust in 1990.

Mary Moran and Eddie Porter, relaxing after a night at the pictures in 1962.

Margaret McAllister remembers the Plaza for a different reason as she recalls her teenage dancing days there with fondness. 'I loved Borderland and the Plaza, and I would go with my friends to one or the other every week without fail. I met Joe Gorman at the Borderland and we were going out for a couple of weeks, you know, to the pictures or just a walk out the road. But one night we had a tiff so we stopped seeing each other.

'In between times I went to the usual dances with my friends again but we seemed to keep missing each other. This Friday night we were debating which dance we would go to. I wanted to go to Borderland, because I thought Joe would be there; he loved Borderland. However, the other two

Annie Reilly and long-time boyfriend Frankie Downey enjoying a lull during a dance at the Plaza in 1966.

wanted to go to the Plaza, so we settled on the Plaza. When we were queuing to leave our coats in the cloakroom, I was delighted when I noticed Joe passing by on his way into the main hall. I was surprised because I thought he would be at Borderland. By this time we had been finished for about four or five weeks. Stuffing our cloakroom tickets inside our shoes, we took up our usual spot on the dance floor.

'The dance was in full swing and we were all enjoying ourselves – we had just finished a jiving set. The next dance was a slow one. As the band struck up, I couldn't believe my eyes when I saw Joe and this fellow I had met a couple of times at previous dances walking towards me. Both arrived beside me at the same time and both put out their hand, the way fellows did when they were asking you to dance. My friends just stood there looking at me with their mouths open. It seemed like an eternity but it was really only a few seconds. I didn't look at the other fellow at all, I just nodded to Joe and we walked onto the floor.

'During that dance we patched up our tiff and stayed together for the rest of the night. That was forty-four years ago and we are still dancing away together to this day.

'But I keep reminding him he just got there in the nick of time!' she laughs.

Charlie Morrison and friends having a ball at the Plaza in 1966.

Angela Friel from Lifford receiving close attention from Finbar McConnell at the Plaza in 1965.

Kathleen McGowan with her boyfriend, all-Ireland boxing champion Patsy Doherty, at the Plaza in Buncrana in 1968.

Breege McCallion and boyfriend Christie Sheerin with friends Charlie and Mary Kelly at the Plaza in 1966.

Michael 'Tutin' Doherty, John 'Noisy' McCallion, Seán Bradley, Joe McCallion, Mike McAllister and Brian Donnelly in a Buncrana bar on a Sunday afternoon and looking forward to the Plaza that night.

Margaret McCauley, Marian Cross and Isobel McGowan at the Embassy in 1967.

Maureen O'Grady and Daphne Doherty at the Embassy with a friend in 1968.

The Trend Showband in the mid-'60s with John O'Hagan on trumpet, Richie Kelly on drums, Eddie Sweeney on sax, Michael O'Doherty on trombone, vocalist Peter 'Boy' Roddy, Hugo Carlin on bass, Johnny Murray on sax and Raymond Beals on guitar.

A Trend Emerges

The Derry showbands of the 1950s and '60s had all but departed the stage, but it wasn't the end of them just yet. News spread of a new, emerging Derry showband full of teenagers and the word was they were good. Talented vocalist Peter 'Boy' Roddy was lead singer and front man of the newly formed Trend Showband. Managed by local personality Eddie Davis, they quickly made a name for themselves and became quite popular in a short time. The band was packed with quality young musicians and their prospects looked rosy; they were pulling in good crowds all over the country and seemed destined for the top. Their talent was obvious and they were offered a tour of Canada. The lure of plying their trade in a new country was a big pull for the young lads, so they naturally accepted the offer and looked forward to challenging and exciting times.

In hindsight, leaving the Irish circuit when they were making such a big impression with promoters may not have been a wise move. On their return home from Canada a few years later, picking up where they left off proved more difficult than anticipated. Later on they changed management to Tony Byrne from Dublin. While they enjoyed some further success on the Irish circuit, many people thought had they stayed at home they could have hit the top. However, for the years they played the circuit they provided first-class enjoyment to audiences far and wide, not least in Derry where they are fondly remembered to this day.

The Derry Beatle

I was walking down Park Avenue when I ran into one of Rosemount's well-known characters, Paddy 'Beatle' McLaughlin. Paddy was a very popular teenager at the dance halls in the mid-'60s, a jovial man by nature and always one with a joke to tell.

While standing talking to him about the topics of the day, a middle-aged woman came out of the Post Office and acknowledged him with the words. 'Yes, Beatle.' A minute later, a young man passed us and just said, 'What about ye, Beatle?'

Curious, I asked him how he came to acquire the nickname Beatle. He laughed loudly as he began to tell me. 'It happened when I was working in the BSR factory at Drumahoe. I worked as an apprentice …'

He stops talking as a man driving past slows down and shouts, 'Beatle, you could talk for Ireland.'

Margaret Billington baby-sitting her niece Coleen Norris. Unknown to her, she was about to meet her life partner Paddy 'Beatle' McLaughlin that night.

Paddy roars back, 'Where are you taking that thing to – Corry's scrap yard?' He then advises the driver in no uncertain terms to go to the credit union, get a loan and buy a decent car! The driver moves on, waving back at Paddy.

'He's a headbin, but good craic,' chuckles Paddy, describing the driver.

'What do you call him?' I ask.

'Haven't a clue,' answers Paddy.

Paddy took up the story back at his house. 'I was an apprentice, but don't ask me an apprentice what! You know the craic. Back then, everyone was an apprentice something or other in the BSR. Anyway, it was mostly women who worked in the Drumahoe factory. I had long hair in the '60s and was always singing Beatles songs while working. Plus the fact that I was probably one of the first in Derry to wear the collarless Beatle suit might've had something to do with it. One day at work a Beatle track came on the radio. I grabbed a sweeping brush that was nearby and started to gyrate and pretend to sing the song. One of the girls shouted out, "Look at the Beatle!" Everyone started calling me Beatle after that.

'Talking about the collarless Beatle suit, I remember the first one I ordered. It was from the Weaver to Wearer clothes shop in Ferryquay Street. Like everybody

175

Jack Cook and the Jackpots serenaded Margaret and Paddy at the Plaza.

else at that time, I was buying it on credit. I paid my deposit, signed my name over the queen's head on a stamp and was duly measured and told it would be ready for collection the following Saturday.

'The morning I was to collect my suit, I bought a pair of Beatle boots and a new shirt and tie to go with it. And with my hair already cut Beatle-style, I was really looking forward to going out that night. Before going up the town to collect the suit, I called in to Dickie Gallagher's bookies and laid a few bets on the horses, which all won. I had a grin on my face as wide as the Foyle as I walked down Creggan Hill on my way to collect my suit.

'However, when I walked through the doors of Weaver to Wearer, I was told my suit hadn't arrived. I was so disappointed, as I intended to wear all my new gear to the dance in the Stardust that night. Mr O'Donnell, the manager, seeing how disappointed I was, told me it still might come in the afternoon. As it was three o'clock, I had all but given up hope of it coming in that Saturday and I was resigned to wearing my old suit that night.

'I was having my supper around six o'clock when I answered a knock on our door. There, standing at my doorstep with my new Beatle suit in his hand, was Mr O'Donnell; he told me it came in five minutes after I left the shop. I thanked him heartily and he left, happy that he had another satisfied customer.

'Up the stairs like a flash I went to try it on. It fitted and matched perfectly with my new boots, shirt and thin tie. I couldn't wait to hit the Stardust.

'Looking in the mirror that night, I thought that Beatle was an apt nickname for me. Some people only know me as 'Beatle' and they even think that's my surname. A man passed me and Margaret, my wife, up the town one day and said, "Yes, Paddy. Hello, Mrs Beatle." He genuinely didn't know that it was my nickname. If someone came to Rosemount and asked where Paddy McLaughlin lived, some of the younger people wouldn't know who they were talking about. But if they asked where Beatle lives, all of them could tell you.'

Paddy's wife Margaret nods her head and says, 'For God's sake, I was going with him for three weeks before I knew his surname was McLaughlin; I thought it was Beatle myself,' she laughs.

Paddy went on to chat about his time at the dances.

'I danced in every square inch of every dance floor within a twenty-mile radius of Derry. You name a dance hall and me and the mates danced in it. We had some great craic then.

'Did I ever tell you about the night me and your friend Smiley (Brendan Wilkinson) were at the British Legion show out the Collon Lane? I can still remember the fight that took place; it was 'Tight' Downey who started the lot,' he said with a serious look on his face.

'But Tight wasn't a fighting man,' I said to Paddy.

Grabbing my arm, he says, 'You don't have to be a fighter to start a fight. Tight came home from working in London and he was dressed like Burton's dummy and full as a kite. The band was playing away and Tight was dancing around the floor on his own, oblivious to everybody. Suddenly, he jumped onto the stage and grabbed the mike out of the singer's hand and started to sing. We all clapped and cheered him for the craic. But Tight just kept on singing and singing and he refused to come down from the stage.

'The organisers, a couple of old boys, were hopping mad and they called the cops. When the cops arrived, all hell broke loose. Some fellow started cheering the cops, who were pulling Tight off the stage, and someone hit him. Then the fists started flying and chairs were hurled through the air; it was sheer bedlam. We were badly outnumbered, so after throwing a few punches, we cleared off in a hurry. A crowd of boys followed us and the only way we could avoid being seen was to lie in the burn, which was full of water. We lay there for about thirty minutes before moving on to the road again and we were soaked and mucked to the eyeballs.

'As we started walking home we saw Tight Downey walking down the road, still singing his head off and not a hair tossed on his head. We told him he had started the fight. He looked at us and was amazed at what we said. "What fight? Who was fighting? I saw no fight," and he just continued on his way, singing at the top of his voice.'

After Paddy's laughter subsided, I asked him where he'd met his wife.

'That's another story. I met her in the Plaza in Buncrana, but she shot me down the first time I asked to get off with her.'

'Why did she do that?' I enquired.

'Because I had long hair and I had it tied in a ponytail. She wasn't at all impressed with it. Me and Gino Delpinto were eyeing up these two women out on the floor. Gino said he would go for the one with the brown hair, which was Margaret. But I told him I wanted to ask her so he agreed to dance with Margaret's friend.

'After she shot me down, she was standing with her friend at the side of the hall. I fancied her, so I decided not to take no for an answer. So back I went and asked her

other dance. This time it was
w dance.

ı asked her why she didn't want to go for a mineral with me. She remained silent, but I knew it was because of my hair. There was this fellow dancing beside us who had a very long nose. I nudged Margaret and said to her, "See that fellow with the long nose? Well, he can't cut it shorter, but I can cut my hair!" She just burst out laughing. I then worked my charm on her and she eventually agreed to go for a mineral with me. Now, if a girl went for a mineral with you back then that usually meant she was going to go off with you.

'I left her home that night and I can remember everything about it as if it was last week! It was Friday 11 August 1967 and the band on stage was Jack and the Jackpots.

'Going up home in the bus, she told me she lived in Westway, which was handy, as I lived close by in Artisan Street in Rosemount. We started dating steady after that and one Sunday night we decided to go on Davy McLaughlin's bingo bus to Buncrana, which left from Rosemount.

Margaret and Paddy McLaughlin on their wedding day, 26 December 1968.

'We had planned just to stroll around the town, as neither of us drank, but it started to rain. So we decided to go into the Plaza where the bingo was being held. As we were there, we decided we might as well play a few games. And would you believe it, we won the snowball, which paid £200, a huge amount of money then. We decided to put it in the bank in a joint account and soon we were planning our wedding.

'We got married on Boxing Day 1968 in St Eugene's Cathedral; our reception was held in the old City Hotel. We had seventy-five guests at our wedding, a steak menu, and the bill for the reception totalled £92.'

Paddy went on to say, 'We went to every dance hall in Derry and half of the venues in Donegal. It was a brilliant era and we had a ball. The showbands and dance halls may be long gone, but the memories live on.'

The Cameo/Stardust

In the week beginning Monday 16 December 1963, the tradesmen of local builder Frank O'Connor were working day and night in a race against the clock. Their aim was to have the Bogside's first purpose-built ballroom in decades ready for the gala opening planned for the following Monday. Just as Frank O'Connor's men left no stone unturned to have this new modern ballroom ready on time, the same can be said of the owners, who had organised a spectacular line-up of top-notch showbands who would supply a superb opening week of entertainment. The Bogside, and indeed the whole of Derry, was buzzing with excitement as the date for the opening of this new venue drew closer. The prospect of seeing international superstars as well as Ireland's top showbands playing in their own back yard was something the young people of the city relished.

So as planned, on Monday 23 December 1963 the Cameo Ballroom opened its doors in a blaze of publicity to the sound of Strabane's showband pioneers, the Clipper Carlton. Also on stage that night was the Derry City Showband. The crowds came in their droves and the ballroom was full to capacity within one hour of opening. The Cameo was owned by the McIvor family from Muff who also owned the massively popular Borderland dance hall.

Betty Doherty and boyfriend Willie McKeever enjoying the atmosphere in the Cameo in 1965.

George Lynch, Harry Ward and James Ward at the Stardust in 1966.

Two nights later, on Christmas night, the legendary Capitol Showband became the first southern band to play there. Eileen Reid and the Cadets took the stage at the first New Year's Eve dance. What a line-up to launch Derry's newest dance hall!

The Derry City Showband opened the New Year on Friday 3 January 1964 and were followed by the popular Woodchoppers soon after. The Cameo and the refurbished Embassy along with the Mem became the three most popular dance halls in Derry for teenagers in the mid- to late '60s. The music was mainly cover versions of the British Top Twenty with the odd showband cover version of an American song, and the *very* odd showband original song.

I can't remember too many country showbands playing Derry, as country music was frowned upon by the city's teenagers and was strictly a no-go. The only one who got away with playing the rare country 'Hooley' song would have been Joe Dolan, simply because he was a class showman. He could get away with the likes of *The Westmeath Bachelor*, as the teenagers treated that as a free-for-all on the dance floor. It was the kind of number when anything and everything was acceptable. Mainly, it would be arms interlocked with your partner and both swinging around the floor at breakneck speed. It was not uncommon for a few couples to end up on all fours on the floor and laughing their heads off.

Joe Dolan's first visit to the Cameo was just a few short weeks after it opened, on Saturday 8 February 1964. The doors were closed early, as the hall was packed to the rafters for the first visit of Mullingar's mega-showband stars. They provided a super show for the dancers and the night was a roller coaster from start to finish. The band certainly sent the dancers home sweating that night. Admission was five shillings, value for money by anyone's standards!

No smoking ban here! Frankie 'Spud' Murphy, Teresa Caldwell and Danny 'Mousey' McLaughlin with dancing partner Etta Maguire at the Embassy in 1971.

The talented Sands Showband, a breakaway from the original Miami showband.

Wilma Frazer, Ann Ivy and Jacqueline Millar at the Embassy in 1969.

Right: One lucky fan gets an autograph from Helen Shapiro after her performance at the Corinthian Ballroom in October 1963.

Below: A group of Derry dancers at the Plaza in Buncrana. Included is Hugh Harkin.

Two young ladies walking up Frederick Street after collecting their tickets to see American legend Roy Orbison performing in the Cameo in 1964. Looking on is a young mother just content to rock her baby to sleep.

Roy Orbison Comes to Town

On Friday 16 July 1965, the young working people of Derry were in jovial mood. Not only was it the weekend, but the annual August holidays – when the shirt factories, building sites, offices and other workplaces would close for two weeks – was nearly upon them. Another reason why some of them were happy that weekend was because world-famous American singing sensation Roy Orbison was in town. And he would be appearing in the Cameo. Even though it was a whopping ten shillings to gain admission, double the normal price, the young people of the city and further afield packed the Cameo on Wednesday 21 July 1965.

Orbison gave a faultless performance that thrilled the dancers, some of whom just stood at the front of the stage and stared at him in awe of his professionalism and sheer class as he belted out his hit numbers like *Pretty Woman*, which sold over seven million copies, *In Dreams*, *Blue Bayou* and *Crying*.

Of course, Roy Orbison was later to become an iconic figure in the music industry throughout the world and is credited with persuading his close friends the Beatles to tour America. People still remember as if it were last year that hot summer night way back in 1965 when he stood on the Bogside stage. Many also recall with fondness how hundreds of young people gathered outside the Cameo, hoping to catch a glimpse of him. Others talked of seeing women and men of all ages hanging out of open windows in the houses that surrounded the Bogside venue, hoping to see him as he entered the venue. The American superstar was one of many international stars to appear in ballrooms in Derry around that time.

WORLD'S NO. 1 HIT MAKER !

ROY ORBISON

"Pretty Woman," "In Dreams," "Blue Bayou," etc., etc.

CAMEO : WED., 21st JULY

ALSO PRESIDENTS SHOWBAND

Dancing : 9—2 a.m.   Admission : Ten Shillings

International star Roy Orbison plays in the Bogside.

The venue went on to host every top showband in Ireland and many chart-topping groups and artists from England. It later changed its name to the Stardust and is mostly remembered by that name by nearly everyone today.

It was a popular venue, especially for the teenagers from the town, because of its proximity to their homes, which made it easily accessible. Parents also liked the fact their children were close at hand on their nights out. The only drawback was that the toilets were situated downstairs, so you had a constant stream of people on the stairs all night. Still, Derry teenagers flocked to the venue and the owners started organising competitions for girls, similar to those held in the Embassy. Popular local girl Attracta Simms was crowned the Stardust Queen on New Year's Day in 1969.

By 1977, the crowds had dwindled to such an extent that the owners took the decision to close it. The parish clergy were of the opinion that if the hall were to close it would be a devastating loss to the young of the area. With this in mind, they met the owners and entered into a five-year lease agreement with an option to purchase. They continued to run dances and changed the name to St Eugene's Parish Hall.

Five years later, they bought the hall outright and Raymond Rogan was installed as manager. It continued to be a venue for different functions, mainly dancing, until it closed in 2006.

Stardust advertising from July and October of 1969.

Some of Derry's finest caught the attention of the Derry Journal *photographer at the Embassy in 1969. From left: Juliette Porter, Kathleen Whoriskey, Sue Doherty, Sheila Sheils, Majella Gibson and Maureen O'Grady.*

The best groundsman in Derry, John McCaul, with Angela Duffy at the Plaza in 1966.

Jean Rafferty and boyfriend, well-known sportsman Colm Norris, pictured at the Plaza Ballroom in 1964.

A 'Large' Drifters' Fan

Charlie Large, a big Joe Dolan fan since he first took to the dance floor in Borderland as a young teenager, remembers Joe Dolan's hit numbers *The Answer To Everything*, his first recording, and *Make Me An Island*. 'When I hear either of those songs they instantly transport me back to my dance-hall and showband days. I loved those songs and Joe Dolan was my favourite singer, and the Drifters my favourite band. They were very popular in Derry.'

Charlie remembers playing about the streets of 'Tintown' in Shantallow with his mates as a teenager. 'I used to play football in the streets with my mates after work and a few of us travelled twice a week to St Eugene's Boys Boxing Club as there were no youth club or community centres then in our area. The Church, seeing that other activities in the area began to influence the young ones, decided to start a club in my old school, St Patrick's in Pennyburn. I, like most of the teenagers around there, joined; actually, I was elected as the first secretary of Pennyburn Boys Club. We needed money to get some new equipment, so we decided to run a dance every Saturday night and it was a great success. Most of the club dances took the format of a disco, often playing the latest releases borrowed from the jukebox of a café owned by the Italian grandfather of my soon-to-be girlfriend Esterina.

Louie Macari, pictured with a customer at his Central café in William Street, which was frequented by most dancers in the 1950s and '60s. Their jukebox was the busiest in the town as teenagers played the hits of the day non-stop.

187

'It was during one of those dances that I first met Esterina. She was a very pretty girl. I was instantly attracted to her and after working up some courage, I asked her to dance. I couldn't wait until a Saturday night came round to attend the dances and see her again. I was fascinated by her; she was so quiet, charming and very well mannered, as well as being very attractive. She lived in the rather swanky and affluent Duncreggan Road area of Derry. I knew straightaway that this was the girl for me. She was of Italian descent; her mother was one of the Macari family, the well-known café owners, who located to Derry from Italy.

Charlie Large with his happy bride Esterina on their wedding day in 1972.

'The showband dances were the highlight of so many people's week back in those days. It was during one of the dances at the hop I asked her if she'd like to go to a real dance in the Pallidrome in Strabane the following Saturday night. She asked me who was playing. Once I told her it was Joe Dolan and the Drifters she instantly agreed, and that was our first big dance. After sampling the atmosphere of a real showband dance, we could never go back to the club hops.

'The hops had played their part in us getting to meet, but it was now time to spread our wings. We said goodbye to them and hello to the big ballrooms. From then on we took to the dance floors of the Embassy, Stardust and Borderland. We loved the great atmosphere all the showbands brought to these dance halls. However, if Joe Dolan and the Drifters were playing anywhere in Ireland, we would try to be there.

'We loved that band and have been lifelong friends with them since the mid-1960s. We would often stay in the same hotel as the lads, sitting chatting into the wee small hours as Joe would unwind after another great performance.

'When Esterina decided it was time for me to meet her parents, I was apprehensive, as I didn't know how I would be received. But to my delight, I was treated as one of the family.

'After that, we were recognised as going steady and within a few months I popped the question. Soon, we got engaged and announced the date for our wedding. We were married in St Patrick's Church in Pennyburn in February 1971. We loved the

188

era we grew up and danced in, as we had the best of times travelling around and enjoying such great music and performers.

'I was in my daughter's home in Long Island, New York, for Christmas 2007 when, on Boxing Day, I received a text message from one of the band about Joe's untimely death. As I sat in shock, Tanya, my daughter, quickly arranged for my flight back to attend his funeral in Mullingar. It was the least I could do for a man who gave us so many good memories and so much pleasure with his music.'

Former Mayor of Derry Mary Bradley wholeheartedly agrees. 'Joe was the type of singer who could bring every song to life and

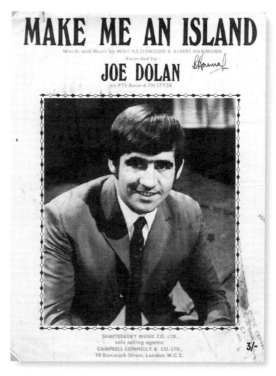

he came across as a humble, kind and caring person, and not one with an ego. When I was privileged to be Mayor of Derry, I was delighted when he agreed to play at my charity ball in the Guildhall. Nobody could ever doubt that Joe Dolan was a true gentleman with the common touch.'

Willie Deery, Brendan 'Smiley' Wilkinson, John Doherty, Seamus Callaghan and Stevie Wilkinson at a hop in Killea Hall in 1964.

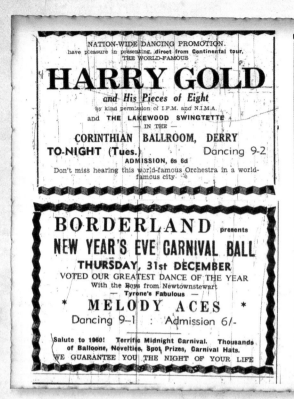

The last dance of the decade, New Year's Eve, 1959.

New Spotlight, June '66

• IRELAND'S TOP 30 FOR MAY •

1. **THE FLY**—Brendan Bowyer and the Royal.
2. **AMONG THE WICKLOW HILLS** — Larry Cunningham and Mighty Avons.
3. **BLACK AND TAN GUN** — The Johnny Flynn Showband.
4. **UP WENT NELSON**—The Go Lucky Four.
5. **ELUSIVE BUTTERFLY** — Val Doonican.
6. **THE SEA AROUND US**—The Ludlow Trio.
7. **DEDICATED FOLLOWER OF FASHION**—Kinks.
8. **BANG BANG**—Cher.
9. **SOUND OF SILENCE** — The Bachelors.
10. **TWO OF A KIND** (E.P.) — The Drifters.
11. **YOU DON'T HAVE TO SAY YOU LOVE ME**—Dusty Springfield.
12. **TURN OUT THE LIGHT** — The Creatures.
13. **PRETTY FLAMINGO** — Manfred Mann.
14. **SLOOP JOHN B.**—The Beachboys.
15. **PIED PIPER**—Crispian St. Peter.
16. **HOLD TIGHT**—Dave Dee, Dozy, Beaky, Mick and Tich.
17. **MAKE THE WORLD GO AWAY** — Eddie Arnold.
18. **THE BALLAD OF THE GREEN BERET**—Sgt. Barry Sadler.
19. **WORRY**—Pat Lynch and the Airchords.
20. **DAYDREAM**—The Lovin' Spoonful.
21. **THE SUN AINT GONNA SHINE** — The Walker Brothers.
22. **NELSON FAREWELL** — The Dubliners.
23. **ABOVE AND BEYOND** — Houston Wells and the Premier Aces.
24. **AMONG THE WICKLOW HILLS** — Gerry Cronin and the Ohio.
25. **SOMEBODY HELP ME** — Spencer Davis.
26. **COME BACK TO STAY** — Dickie Rock and the Miami.
27. **LOVELY LEITRIM** — Larry Cunningham and the Mighty Avons.
28. **BLACK AND TAN GUN** (E.P.)— Sean Dunphy and Hoedowners.
29. **ALFIE**—Cilla Black.
30. **SHOWBAND AROUND THE CORNER**—Art Supple and the Victors.

Based on NEW SPOTLIGHT'S weekly returns for the Month of May.

STARDUST CLUB

Tomorrow (Saturday)   LATE LATE SHOW

DERRICK & THE SOUNDS

Christmas Night   Dancing 9—2   Admission 10/-

CANDY

St. Stephen's Night   Dancing 9—2   Admission 8/-

CLOUDS

Saturday, 27th December   LATE LATE SHOW

TRIXONS

New Year's Eve   Dancing 9—2   Admission 10/-

John Farrell and the DREAMS

Saturday, 3rd January   LATE LATE SHOW

Plattermen

The Chairman and Committee would like to wish our members and friends a Merry Christmas and a Happy New Year

The last dance of the decade, New Year's Eve, 1969.

Joe McKinney, Marian Barr, Margaret Doherty (partly hidden) and Bertie Barrett sharing a joke and downing a few pints before moving on to the Stardust in 1973.

New Year's Eve Dances

The New Year's Eve dances were, for most, the highlight of the dancing calendar; everyone went out that night. It was important to get down to your chosen venue early, as large crowds would be queuing, irrespective of which showband was playing. There was always a carnival atmosphere with scores of balloons in nets suspended from the ceiling over the dance floor. After eleven o'clock, the excitement would increase, because every fifteen minutes the lead singer in the band would announce how many minutes it was until midnight. With one minute to go, the band would stop playing and begin the countdown: ten, nine, eight ... and at the stroke of midnight, the chimes of Big Ben would be relayed by radio through the sound system. The balloons would be released and this was the cue for bedlam to erupt on the dance floor. It would take about fifteen minutes for things to calm down again and everyone to resume the serious business of trying to get off. It was considered a disaster if you didn't succeed on New Year's Eve night.

William Street would be packed with New Year's revellers after the Embassy and the Stardust were over. The craic while waiting in the queue at Duddy's fish-and-chip shop was something else. The girls working behind the counter certainly earned their money on those nights.

192

Willie Deery and wife Betty at a friend's wedding in 1976, just two weeks after they themselves had got married.

Leaving Mates and Meeting Partners

It was in the summer of 1969 when Stevie Wilkinson and Yours Truly had our first ever holiday. I remember we were attending my sister Theresa's wedding to Henry Doherty. After the reception in the Telstar in Creggan, we caught the bus from Foyle Street to Dublin. While we were strolling along O'Connell Street, we noticed a group of Derry girls who were also on holiday there. In that group of girls was Shelia McBride, later to become Stevie's wife. We stopped to talk and got a photograph taken with them, after which we went our separate ways.

Stevie was to meet Shelia a few years later at the Point Inn. This time, they chatted and danced and started dating and were married a couple of years later.

However, I was the first to depart our group of mates as I started going out with a girl from Ardmore.

Stevie Wilkinson and I were enjoying the band at the Embassy Ballroom one Saturday night in February 1970. We were dancing as if no-one else was on the floor and I bumped into this young black-haired girl. The bump was severe enough that I felt I needed to apologise, but she laughed it off. The next dance I saw her standing with this fellow but I didn't think they were together, so I nodded to her, the kind of nod that says, do you want to go out to dance? She smiled back and shrugged her shoulders, gesturing she was with another fellow.

The following week with Stevie and Bertie Barrett, I went to the Stardust. Halfway through the night, I spotted the same dark-haired girl; this time she was dancing with a female friend. It was a fast dance, so, being cute, I decided to bide my time until there was a slow one. When the next slow set came up I made a beeline for her and we were soon smooching around the floor. Her name was Betty Crawford and she remembered me from the previous week at the Embassy. I played it cool and said, 'Ah, I remember you now. You nearly knocked me off my feet.'

'I think it was the other way about,' she replied.

Everyone's first holiday! Willie Deery, Sally Healy, Stevie Wilkinson, Pauline Beattie, Frances Beattie, Sheila McBride and Theresa Millar in Dublin, 1969.

After the slow set was over, I asked her to stay on for the fast set and she agreed. On the next slow set, I asked her where she lived. 'Ardmore,' she replied.

My heart sank. That's a hundred miles away, I thought to myself.

'That's far away,' I said.

'We get a taxi home from Foyle Taxis in Foyle Street,' she said. Hearing that made me feel better, so we then made our way up to the balcony of the Stardust and sat down at a table and had a mineral.

I walked her to her taxi in Foyle Street and we decided we would meet on Monday night and go to the pictures. After that we went to dances in the Stardust, Borderland and the Embassy, and during the week, we attended the pictures, the normal routine for couples then. We also took advantage of the fact that Betty was working in an office in Derry to meet up during the day at lunch times when work permitted.

Sheila McBride and Stevie Wilkinson looking happy after returning from their honeymoon.

My mates were down at my house looking for me on several occasions, but I was never in, as I was dating now. I hadn't seen them for three weeks and then we ran into them at Borderland one night. Stevie informed me they had a search party out looking for me! That was the end of running with my mates from then on. Betty and I were now going steady.

We got married in 1976 and had our reception in Keaveney's Hotel in Moville. Over one hundred guests celebrated with us and the music was supplied by the Bannermen (formerly the Coasters) featuring the multitalented Bonnar brothers. We spent the first night of our honeymoon at the Inter Counties Hotel in Lifford.

The next day we drove to Dublin where we spent the rest of our honeymoon. After breakfast on the first morning, we decided to drive to Bray in nearby County Wicklow. We walked to where we parked our car the previous night and got the first shock of our married life. We found our car, which we'd borrowed from Betty's family, had been stolen. Thankfully, the Gardaí got it back a few hours later, minus a few parts. After getting a mechanic to fix it, we continued on our honeymoon without any further hitches.

Colm McLaughlin and his girlfriend Eileen McLaughlin were regular dance-goers as seen here in 1974.

Eugene O'Donnell and his girlfriend Siobhan Carlin are all smiles at a Stardust dance in 1973.

Joe McKinney and Bertie Barrett are trying to remember what they got up to the night before back in 1974.

Derry all-girl band the Cheries with manager Bob Barron. Included are the Mallett sisters.

Bridie Murray and boyfriend Neil McCafferty at the Stardust in 1973.

These two showband men having a chat in Canada in 1970 are John Deehan and Johnny Murray.

The very popular Trade Winds who rocked the Point Inn for thirteen years: Sam Kelly,
Tony Molloy, Joan McGeady (née Boyle) and Michael MacCafferty.

The Legendary Trade Winds

Whenever the Point Inn is mentioned by former patrons, the first thing that usually springs to mind would be the Trade Winds. Although not a showband, it would be remiss of me not to mention them. Considered by many to be the best folk group to come out of Derry, they were ever-present on the entertainment scene in the North West. They enthralled the crowds with their enthusiasm and their own special brand of music.

And such was their popularity that their weekend residency in the very popular Quigley's Point venue in County Donegal lasted for over thirteen years.

The quartet, made up of Joan McGeady (née Boyle), Tony Molloy, Sam Kelly and Michael MacCafferty, were playing almost nightly until the tragic and untimely death of Joan. The sheer joy they brought to the people of the North West over those years can never be quantified. Their time at the Point Inn is now legendary and has never been forgotten by the music-loving public.

Above: Miss Teen Derry final of 1967: Sheila Sheils, runner-up, Patricia McNulty, winner, and in third place, Margaret Anderson. Also pictured is Embassy manager Robert Ferris.

Below: These young ladies are having a great time at the Embassy in 1969. Included is Pauline Ross.

Sitting comfortably at the Embassy in 1968 are Dorothy Robinson, Linda McNulty and Joan Lynch.

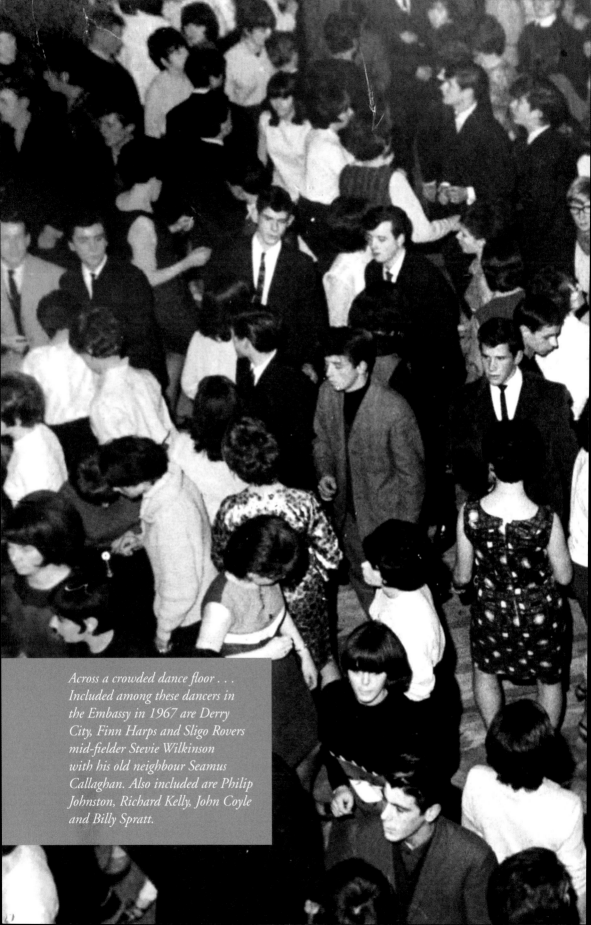

*Across a crowded dance floor . . .
Included among these dancers in
the Embassy in 1967 are Derry
City, Finn Harps and Sligo Rovers
mid-fielder Stevie Wilkinson
with his old neighbour Seamus
Callaghan. Also included are Philip
Johnston, Richard Kelly, John Coyle
and Billy Spratt.*

Ready for a good night of dancing in the Embassy in 1966 are Lila Sheerin, Gordon Thornton and Roseanna Sheerin.

Ladies' Choice

Ladies' choice was at one time a popular and regular feature of the local dances. A man's ego would be greatly boosted if an attractive lady came over to him and asked him to dance. However, just because a lady asked you to dance it didn't necessarily mean she fancied you, as Liam Harkin explains.

'The ladies'-choice dances could prove a bit misleading. When a girl came over and asked a man to dance, it was natural for him to assume all he had to do was invite her to go for a mineral and that was him off, but that was not always the case. Because the woman sometimes was only using the man to make the man she *really* fancied jealous. I know boys who thought the girl fancied them and later went over to dance the girl. When they asked if there was any chance of leaving her home, they were often shot down flat.'

Joe McLaughlin nodded his head in agreement before adding, 'That's right enough, but some women have a strange way of telling you they fancy you, and there were some snobby women about then.'

That took us on to another sore point with the men as we went on to list some of the girls we thought were snobby and wouldn't dare ask to dance for fear of refusal. We now know that the confident, assured girls were never snobby and would never refuse a man a dance. Being refused a dance was, above all, the most embarrassing thing that could happen to a fella. And I am sure it has happened to most of the men who frequented the dance halls, although maybe not as much in the '50s as in the '60s or '70s. Being refused a dance had the potential of ruining a man's night, and if you didn't enjoy the dance, then the whole weekend was a bit of a damp squib.

Jim Doherty remembers one such occasion in the Castle in Dungiven when it was very noticeable, as it was the start of the night.

'With the men slow to start dancing, this young fella went over and asked a girl out to dance, but she refused. The showband on stage that night was the Cadets. Eileen Reid and the rest of the band could not but notice this. After the set of songs were over, one of the band members grabbed the microphone from Eileen Reid and said, "Ladies, please remember, this is a dance hall and we are all here to dance and enjoy ourselves." You could hear a pin drop in the hall as he handed the microphone back to Eileen Reid. It was a simple statement that had its desired effect immediately. A young lady, within seconds of the next number being played by the band, walked across the floor and asked the young man in question to dance. It was a nice touch and it didn't go on unnoticed, as she was danced off her feet the whole night by practically every male in the hall.

'It has to be said that this incident differs from a girl refusing a man a dance if in her opinion he was too intoxicated; that is understandable. Some girls rightly and steadfastly refused to dance with men who were obviously the worse for wear from drink.'

Regular Stardust dancers: Patsy Quigley, Noreen McGinty and Roseanna Sheerin in 1967.

*Hoping for big things are these girls selected for Miss Derry in 1970. Front:
Ann Carter, Ann Devenney and Mary Smith. Back: Kathleen Wallace, Irene
Collins and Bernadette Harrison.*

These smiling teenagers, Margaret McKeever, Celine Quigley, Sheila Sheils and Christine Brown, were selected to take part in one of the many competitions at the Embassy in 1968.

Three young ladies making an impression at the Embassy in 1970.

Theresa Monaghan, Elizabeth McCallion and Majella McGill enjoying a night out at the Embassy in 1967.

No Hanky-Panky

While sitting chatting to Bertie Barrett in his house at Sandbank Cottages, a friend of Bertie's called in to see him. Having a cup of tea, the three of us got talking about showbands and our dancing days, each reminiscing about our experiences. Bertie's friend related to us this story about his cousin's beloved mother, just to emphasise how innocent people and things were back in those days.

'My cousin left Derry to go and work in Dublin where he met a girl. Like him, she was living in a rented flat. After they got to know each other they decided to move into the one place and share the cost. They also started going out and soon were an item. My cousin always phoned his mother every Sunday and during one of these calls he decided to tell her about

Siobhan Carlin, Eugene O'Donnell, Marian Barr, Brendan Wilkinson, Maureen McHugh and Sheila McBride at a wedding.

Mary. Immediately, his mother said she hoped there was no hanky-panky going on. He assured her there wasn't and it was purely a business arrangement, as they shared the rent of the flat. He told her Mary and he had separate rooms.

'The following Sunday as usual he duly phoned his mother; again the conversation turned to Mary. Once again he assured his mother that there was nothing going on and told her she would just have to trust him. Two weeks later, his mother said she would like to visit him and he told her she was very welcome to do so. The next week, his mother arrived and stayed for two nights. While there, his mother slept in his bed, Mary slept in her own bed and he slept on the couch. All went well and at last she seemed happy enough with the arrangements my cousin had told her so she returned to Derry.

'However, that night, my cousin noticed a vase was missing from the hall table. Phoning his mother that Sunday as normal, he happened to mention to her that the vase was missing. "Oh, that nice wee vase that was on the hall table?" asked his mother. He told her yes, that was the one, thinking she may have broken it and forgotten to say. And he went on to tell her that Mary has searched the flat from top to bottom looking for it.

'Again she asked, "Are you sure, son, there is no hanky-panky going on between you and Mary?" He again assured her there was nothing going on.

'There was a little silence and then she said, "Well, son, you just tell Mary that if she looks under the blankets on her bed she will find the vase."'

Bertie's friend went on to tell us that Mary and his cousin are now married thirty-seven years and have six children and eight grandchildren!

Roy Arbuckle, The Wild Rover

A lot has been said so far about the dancers, but what about the musicians who provided the entertainment for us for so long? One of those musicians was Roy Arbuckle, former guitarist with the Woodchoppers and Flingels showbands.

Roy's first band was the Swingtones, under band leader Victor Campbell. The band charged £12 per gig, and the fee was divided between the four members and Victor, with the other £2 going towards the petrol.

Roy takes up the story: 'I was the first bass player in Derry to have my own amp, thus making me very popular with sound-conscious band leaders. With Frankie Robinson, Jackie Boyd and Trevor Keys, I formed the Signets. Although I was playing four nights a week, I still held on to my day job in Derry Vision where I repaired televisions. Soon, the strain of two jobs was proving too much, so I knew I had a decision to take. That decision was made for me when John Trotter, a friend and a musician of note, called to my home and offered me a job in Dublin at fifteen pounds a week. I duly left my day job and along with John and Patsy McGinley, I headed off to Dublin to play with Maisie McDaniels and the Fendermen. Maisie was a big name on the showband scene then and she had a weekly slot on RTÉ.

'We settled into digs in Dublin and played in every nook and cranny in Ireland. About a year later, our landlady asked us to leave, as the local priest objected to the string of women we were bringing home after the gigs. We not only left our digs but decided to leave the Fendermen as well and return to Derry.

'I wasn't without work long, as I was asked to join the Woodchoppers, which I did. It was with Willie Bradley's Woodchoppers that I got the opportunity to travel, as the band had a tour of America and Canada lined up. In Canada, we played the famous Maple Leaf Ballroom. Then we journeyed down to New York and were booked into a fancy hotel downtown. Things were looking good and we were enjoying the good life in our plush surroundings in the city that never sleeps. Suddenly things took a turn for the worse.

'While enjoying dinner in the tranquil restaurant of our hotel, we heard a commotion in the foyer. All of a sudden, the restaurant doors were flung open and in rushed about ten officials from the emigration department. They immediately approached our table and politely asked each member of the band to produce their work permits. None of us could. Unfortu-

208

Included in this quartet are Roy Arbuckle and his long-standing friend, legendary drummer Jackie Molloy.

nately, the promoter who brought us to Canada and America didn't go through the correct procedures and we were in the country illegally. The officials were very friendly and, although apologising, explained that under immigration laws, there was no other course available to them but to quietly demand that the band accept voluntary deportation. We had no option but to agree with their 'request.' I think this action was forced upon them simply because of the major publicity our show-band was receiving in the New York press. To be honest, every paper carried at least a half-page story on us and we felt like, and were treated like, the Beatles.

'We were escorted to the airport and put on a plane bound for Ireland. We re-turned to Derry with our egos boosted by the publicity we received, but now it was back to barn-type hallrooms and changing in our van. However, the taste of the high living in America and Canada had an impact on me. Soon after returning to Derry, I decided to emigrate to America, this time legally.

'For years I played with Gerry O'Neill in a two-piece called Fiddler's Elbow. We were very successful and usually played the same venue for two weeks at a time. We played the circuit from Detroit, Nova Scotia, Chicago and Montréal, and although I enjoyed it, the travelling was gruelling.

'Then I went through a very rough time: my girlfriend died. Her untimely death had a severe effect on me and prompted me to have a long, hard look at my lifestyle. I decided there and then something had to change, and I knew I was the only one

The Woodchoppers with a young Roy Arbuckle, shortly before they were deported from New York in 1967.

who could bring about that desired change. So from that day on, I decided the days of all work and no pleasure were over for me and I left Gerry. I took several weeks out from music and just took things easy; I needed to, as I was mentally and physically drained.

'Several weeks later as I was walking down the street, I ran into an old music pal, Noel Lenihan. We went for a pint and Noel asked me if I'd consider joining up with him. After a few more pints I told him I would, but on one condition: it would not be all work and no pleasure. Noel said, "I'm your man." So after sorting out some personal details, we decided to just drift across America. And I mean the whole of the United States, from Montana to New York and back. We played two or three gigs a week and had a ball the rest of the time. The name of our band was appropriate – the Rambling Boys of Pleasure.'

Roy came home for a holiday in the mid-1980s with every intention of returning to settle in Oregon. But the pull of his hometown was too much and he decided to stay in Derry. The man who travelled each and every highway finally decided his rambling days were over.

Would he do it all over again? I queried. After a moment of reflection, hand on chin and looking straight at me, he replied. 'Yes. I believe I probably would, because I did it the way I wanted to do it, not necessarily the right way, but my way.'

The popular Checkers Showband with Michael Roddy, Brendan McCrossan, Seamus Downey and Pat McCrossan.

A Sax Player and a Gentleman

Seamus Downey was the sax player with the Magnificent Seven and the Checkers showbands among others. Seamus was another Derry musician who may have taken the American trail had he not got married. He chuckles as he begins to tell me the story of how he met his wife, Alice Sheils.

Alice, who was in the kitchen, heard the chuckles of Seamus and came into the living room to see what he was laughing about. He informs her he was just telling me about how they met. Alice smiles as she sits down and takes over the story of how they first got together.

'I went to the pictures in the Palace one Monday night with my friends. We settled into our seats and opened our bag of sweets, waiting for the film to start. This fellow, who was obviously looking for a laugh, picked up a fire-extinguisher and pulled the pin and the foam squirted all over the place. We thought he must be a nutcase and to tell you the truth, he scared the life out of us. We didn't know what he was going to do next, so we asked Seamus if he'd sit beside us.

'We got talking and I thought he was a nice, sensible fellow and not bad looking, either. After the film was over, he offered to walk us home and we gladly accepted his offer. When we got to my door, he asked me if I'd like to go to the pictures with him some time. I liked him, and he obviously liked me, so we arranged to meet that Thursday night. It was then that he told me he played in a showband. When he wasn't playing we would go to a dance. Soon, we were seeing each other nearly every night and we then got engaged and married the following year. That was nearly forty years ago. How time flies!'

Seamus went on to say: 'I loved playing the saxophone and when I got the opportunity to join a showband I jumped at the chance. At times it was hard, travelling long hours in dodgy vans, but to be honest, I'd do it all again today, for I loved every minute of it.'

NEW SPOTLIGHT
ANNUAL

Contributed by Liam O'Reilly

IRISH-SHOWBANDS.COM

Left: Some of the lead singers of the Irish showbands who entertained us throughout that great era.

Below: Eight of the best line up with eyes on the Miss Derry title in 1968. Included are Philomena Sheerin, Daphne Doherty and Angela O'Doherty.

*Marie Donnelly, Mary McAllister and Veronica Cavanagh
enjoying the atmosphere at the Embassy in 1968.*

Organised Bedlam But Fun

Marquees provided a major addition to the social lives of many young people during the summer months in rural Ireland. These were just gigantic tents pitched in the middle of a field. Even so, they drew large crowds of holiday-makers and people from far and near. One very popular one with the Derry dancers was the Culdaff marquee, which was held every July and August. Buses leaving Great James Street would be packed on a Sunday night and the craic would be something else. Regulars would be Charlie 'Nucker' Tierney, Tony Nash, Bernard 'Junior' Bradley, Bertie Barrett, Stevie Wilkinson and Yours Truly.

All the top showbands of the day played in the marquees. What made the marquee in Culdaff so popular was the fact that the dancers came from miles around to attend. Busloads converged on the tiny village of Culdaff. They came from Buncrana, Carndonagh, Clonmany and from nearly every village in County Donegal. Also, the Scottish brogue would be very much evident, as there were always large Scottish contingents there on holiday. With dancers from a variety of places, this gave the marquee a marvellous carnival atmosphere.

Conditions inside the marquee could be best described as primitive and toilet facilities were practically nonexistent: you had to walk across a mucky field to get to one. When the dance floor, which was just floorboards laid on top of the grass, was full with dancers, the place really rocked and you literally felt the ground move beneath your feet! On a wet night, it would not have been uncommon to feel the rain drip on your head while dancing. The lights would flicker all night, as the electricity for the band and the lighting was powered by a generator at the rear of the marquee. But all those small things went unnoticed by the dancers once the showband started playing.

Usually, they were so crowded it was just a free-for-all. I suppose you could say it was organised bedlam. But dancers never complained; they were having a ball.

As with many other out-of-town dances, the odd person missed the bus back to Derry. But with Culdaff being a long way from Derry, and with the chances of thumbing a lift on the quiet country roads of County Donegal somewhat remote, most made sure of being on the bus home. Unless, of course, you got off with a Marilyn Monroe look-alike. I do recall at times the bus driver waiting on a few girls only to be told they had got off with some local lads who had cars.

There was the odd marquee in County Derry, but most of the larger ones were down south. Buses left Derry to the ballrooms and marquees from Patrick Street and Great James Street, most of which always had a decent crowd on board with the smell of perfume and Old Spice filling the air.

Another favourite spot on a Sunday night was the Castle in Dungiven. It was always packed to the rafters with dancers, mainly from County Derry. The owner was Jim McCloskey, a nice and humble man. Jim, many years later, told me the most popular acts to play at the Castle in his time were Joe Dolan and the Drifters, and Eileen Reid and the Cadets.

Official Health and Safety concerns at the dances in the showband era were not as vigorously addressed as they are today and the promoters' mantra 'Pack Them In' seemed to be taken literally! Actually, Jimmy Kelly reveals the record for attendance at a ballroom in the North West must surely go to Borderland which Jimmy managed. When Joe Dolan and the Drifters played there on September 1968, there was a crowd of over 4,200, an amazing number when you consider the size of Borderland. Jimmy remembers ventilation was courtesy of all the exit doors being flung fully open to let air in.

Despite the hassle of queuing, the fact that when you did manage to get in, one thing was certain; everyone would have an absolute ball. There was never a prima-donna attitude from the showbands as they put their heart and soul into performing on stage; their motto was 'send them home sweating'. And no-one ever complained that they didn't perform the cover songs as good as the original artists because the atmosphere was always electric.

Borderland

If a survey was carried out among the dancers of the 1950s, '60s, or '70s into what was their favourite ballroom/dance hall, it would be fair to say Borderland would come out on top.

The atmosphere in Borderland was something that would be difficult to describe to someone who did not sample it first-hand. The very name conjures

Borderland advertising from 1975.

up so many happy and fond memories to the young people of that period. When you mentioned Borderland to someone, they would inevitably recount their own personal memory of it. Everyone who danced there has a story to tell of the place. And you cannot talk about Borderland without the names of various bands arising because it was, of course, synonymous with the great showband era.

In the days when not many people had cars, the main conveyance to the hall was by buses which left from Patrick Street every Friday and Sunday night. Buses, especially in the hall's early days, would also come from all over Donegal. They normally pulled up outside Borderland to let the people off and some, mostly male, would immediately head in the direction of the Squealing Pig pub, because the dance halls didn't sell alcohol. The girls would queue up to enter the hall as soon as they disembarked and the drivers parked their buses in the car park at the rear of Borderland. The girls would take their coats to the cloak room then claim their plastic chairs and line them up against the wall at their usual spot every dance night. Now it was just a matter of dancing with their female pals while the relief band played and wait for the big band to come on stage, at which time the men would be all in the hall after getting tanked up in the Squealing Pig.

This same ritual was played out every Friday and Sunday night for many years.

As you'd imagine, every top showband played Borderland: Johnny Quigley's All Stars, the Woodchoppers, Brendan Bowyer and the Royal, Joe Dolan and the Drifters, Dickie Rock, and later Fran O'Toole and the Miami, along with the Freshmen and the Capitol.

Most Derry folk went to Borderland on a Friday night – it was *the* big night of the week – and it was always chock-a-block. Room to dance, especially for

A smiling Connie Cooper in a happy mood as she and steady boyfriend Dan Hegarty enjoy each other's company at a dance in Borderland in 1964.

the jivers, was at a premium, and a slow or close dance was just that, as you were packed in like sardines. Of course, people were not slow to point out that this had its advantages, depending on who was your dancing partner. Literally thousands of marriages emanated from those dances in Borderland.

One of those was the marriage of Tommy Donnelly from William Street and Ardmore girl Maura Ward. Tommy remembers the night he met his wife of forty-seven years vividly.

'I was at Borderland with my usual gang of mates; it was the winter of 1963. We were all standing in a group at one side of the hall, eyeing up the talent as we normally did. Mike McAllister pointed to two girls dancing in the middle of the floor and suggested to me we dance them. "Lead the way," I said to him, and off we went and tapped them on the shoulder and started dancing with them. Halfway through the set, Mike turned to me and said, "Will you dance with this one, she's very cheeky? And I'll take yours." I told him to stay where he was, as it was only a dance. He insisted we change partners, so to keep the peace, I agreed and we swapped over. I got talking to the girl and we got on well together. I enjoyed her company so much I went back and asked her for another dance. Again we got on like a house on fire, so I decided there and then to ask off with her. She agreed and I took her for a mineral. It was then I found out her name and where she lived. We made a further date and arranged to go to the pictures. And that was the end of my single days. Like other couples, we went to dances in most of the halls in or near Derry.'

Joe McCallion, one of his mates, said, 'We all knew from flag fall he was smitten; it was written all over his face. We all envied him because Maura was not only a stunningly attractive woman but also very charismatic. So the only route he was travelling was down the aisle of Ardmore Church.'

And he was right. Tommy and Maura were married in 1965 and after forty-six years they are still happy and contented. Like most other couples of that era, after reminiscing of days gone by, both agreed it was a wonderful time to be young. And they wouldn't swap the memories they have of those years for a winning lotto ticket.

Borderland was the favoured dance hall of two well-known and popular Derry teachers, Paddy Doherty and Philomena Patton, who taught at the North West Technical College and

Tommy Donnelly and Maura Ward at the Pallidrome in Strabane in 1964.

St Brecan's School respectively. Both Paddy and Philomena enjoyed reminiscing with me about their dancing days and how and when they met.

Like most couples, their accounts differ ever so slightly. Both admit, however, that Philomena had little or no grasp of the delicacies of country music until she met Paddy. Philomena, a student at Thornhill College, was an avid '60s pop-group fan and grew up to the Merseybeat sound of the Beatles and Searchers before being converted to the big showband sound. Paddy, although a showband fan, was also partial to the slower pace and gentler side of country music.

Philomena said, 'I never knew much about the showbands until the day I was told by my school friends that one of the girls was mad about a certain Joe Dolan. At first I thought he was just some fella from Derry that she had a crush on until I was informed he was a big showband singing star. So I was really curious about this Irish superstar and when we saw him advertised in the *Derry Journal* for playing at Borderland, we all decided we would go and look him over, so to speak.

'So on that particular Friday we donned our glad rags and off we all went to see him. As we boarded the Borderland bus at Patrick Street, I just didn't have a clue what to expect, as it was my very first showband dance. I, with my friends, went with an open mind but not expecting too much, as after all we were not going to see the Beatles. But I have to admit, I was absolutely gobsmacked, as Joe Dolan and the Drifters were simply brilliant. What an atmosphere, what a sound, and the sheer excitement of the audience as he took to the stage was something I will never forget. We danced close to the stage all night and we had a fantastic time. I became an instant convert to the showband sound and dances that night.

Big smiles all round from these three Clippers before going on stage to a packed hall at Borderland in 1962.

Barry Mallett, Joe McCallion and Danny McCallion are looking confident in Borderland in 1962.

'We raved about the dance to our friends all that week. Now our whole class was buzzing with excitement and planning to go to a showband dance the following weekend.

'Although the Beatles, the Rolling Stones, the Searchers and their like were all very good to watch and listen to on *Top of the Pops*, they simply were no match for the big, live, brass-dominated sound of the showbands.'

Paddy nods his head in approval and went on to say, 'Philomena is right about that, and I also loved the big showbands; Brian Coll was one of my favourites. I just loved the choice of songs he sang and the sound that came from his band, the Plattermen.

Then Rob Strong's influence in the band increased and they went off the beat a bit as far as I was concerned. I wasn't a big fan of Rob Strong; he brought a different sound to the Plat-

Popular student teachers Paddy Doherty and Philomena Patton enjoying the band at Borderland in 1972.

termen. I suppose I can only describe it as a harder type of sound, of the Blood Sweat and Tears stuff. No, definitely not my kind of music at all. I was delighted when Brian Coll left them to set up his other country showband, the Buckaroos, and revert back to his original style and music.

'Now for the story of how Philomena and me met. We were both studying to be teachers and the Troubles were raging at the time in Derry. Both of us were observing one of the riots from a vantage point. But when the action got a little too close for comfort, we decided to leave in a hurry. I had a car and I offered Philomena and her two friends a lift home. I deliberately left Philomena off last and as she was getting out of my car, I asked her if she'd like to meet again, maybe go to the pictures. She agreed and we got on like a house on fire. At the weekend we went to Borderland to hear Butch Moore and the Capitol.

'We went everywhere together after that and like most couples, it was the pictures during the week and then a dance at the weekend. We are now married thirty-seven years and we still like to hear the old showband songs on the Seán Coyle show. We were young at a time when not only the music and dress were changing massively, but the world around us.

'One thing is certain: like everyone else of that era, we were left with plenty of great memories.'

The Fiesta Ballroom, Letterkenny, was a popular venue with Derry dancers.

The Fiesta

The Fiesta was another ballroom frequented on many occasions by Derry dancers whenever their favourite showband was playing there. The Fiesta opened its doors on Friday 5 October 1962 and a crowd in excess of 2,000 packed in to the Letterkenny venue to hear Butch Moore and the Capitol Showband. The ticket price of ten shillings was the entrance fee for this historic night in County Donegal entertainment history. The popular Keaney family were the owners of this impressive new venue. Among the crowd on that first night was a young Letterkenny teenager, John Baird. I asked John if he remembered anything about that first night.

'Remember anything about it?' he laughs. 'I remember every single minute of it. The whole town was buzzing all that week and every young and not-so-young person was counting the hours until the Fiesta opened. It was the topic of conversation in every workplace and indeed every school. The chemist shops ran out of Brylcreem and perfume and the dry-cleaners had a queue a mile long that Friday. When Butch Moore and the Capitol finally took the stage that night, I'm not kidding you, there was enough electricity in the atmosphere to light up the whole of Derry for a month!'

John holds fond memories of his favourite dance hall where he enjoyed many a great night during his teenage years. Mind you, there was no cheek-to-cheek or close dancing allowed in the Fiesta. Getting too close to your partner on the floor was enough to warrant a tap on the shoulder and be politely but firmly told to 'cool it' by one of the stewards. If you failed to heed such warnings, you ran the risk of getting evicted from the ballroom.

One such memory that was extra special to John was the time he went to hear Johnny McEvoy play there. That was the night he asked pretty young Fahan girl June McCarron to dance. They hit it off straightaway and spent the rest of the evening chatting and getting to know each other.

The Capitol Showband on stage on opening night at the Fiesta Ballroom in Letterkenny.

From then on it was June and John, and his mates had to take a back seat, as he was now going steady. John and June were later married and they still live in Letterkenny.

Throughout the early and mid-1970s, the closure of the ballrooms everywhere was growing apace and all too soon it was the Fiesta's time to bow out. On the Friday night of 23 February 1979 there was sadness in the air as Susan McCann and the Storytellers took the stage at the Fiesta Ballroom. It was to be the last dance in this fine venue where many a romance had blossomed and led to marriage. However, although now long gone, it has never been forgotten.

A few years later, John Baird, an authority not only on the history of the Fiesta but on Irish dance halls and showbands in general, decided it was time that the old ballroom took its rightful place in the history of Letterkenny. He thought it would be nice for the mothers, fathers, grandmothers and grandfathers to have one last look back on their old ballroom days. And at the same time, the youth of the area could read about their town's recent past and get a feel for what they were missing.

So John put pen to paper and wrote a marvellous book about his favourite ballroom, the Fiesta. It is now treasured by everyone who bought it. John's book is the definitive record regarding the Fiesta Ballroom, Letterkenny. It will be there to read for many decades to come, and both young and old can sit back, relax and find out all about the place where their parents and grandparents first met. His

222

book can also be used as a valuable reference guide when seeking information regarding the dance halls in and around Letterkenny.

It is only fair John should have the last word on the subject and he had this to say.

'The Fiesta had everything; it had the best bands in the country, it was spacious, had a great atmosphere, friendly staff and great people who owned it. To me, it was the best-run ballroom in the country. As far as the showbands who played there, and there were some great bands, they came from every county and town in Ireland. But I will tell you one thing, there was never a bad showband that came out of Derry. However, I would have to admit the Capitol Showband were my own favourite band.'

The Fiesta's holiday-period programme for August 1963.

The twist gang includes John Duffy and Frankie Campbell with Helen Fitzpatrick, Patricia Duffy and Olive McGinty in 1967.

The opening night of the Fiesta Ballroom in Letterkenny on Friday 5 October 1962.

The Draw of the Showbands

Dance halls were normally packed to the rafters for the showband performances from the mid-1950s until the early 1970s. From the mid-'70s, however, people started to leave the halls in their droves. By 1974, the numbers attending were very small by comparison. Borderland, for instance, in that year went from a high of 2,487 to a low of just 500. To get an idea of just how large the crowds were at the showband dances, one only has to note some of the official attendance figures at Borderland and the Stardust for 1974 shown below. One should also remember that these numbers were around half of what was normal for the mid-1960s.

BORDERLAND
April 1974
Friday 5 – Dickie Rock, 1,435
Friday 12 – Good Friday, No Dance
Easter Sunday – Chips, 1,957
Friday 19 – Horslips, 2,487
Friday 27 – Joe Dolan and the Drifters, 2,173

May 1974
Friday 3 – Candy, 1,143
Friday 10 – Plattermen, 1,857
Friday 17 – Memories, 1,749
Friday 24 – Fran O'Toole and the Miami, 1,614

December 1974
Friday 6 – Sands, 1,487
Friday 13 – Freshmen, 1,891
Christmas Night – Chips, 2,185
New Year's Eve – Memories, 2,703

Admission to all the above dances, including New Year's Eve, was 70p. The record attendance at a dance in Borderland was held by Joe Dolan and the Drifters with 4,200 in September 1968. Indeed, it is worth noting that recorded attendance figures for any Joe Dolan appearance at Borderland never fell below 2,000. They were the only showband ever to achieve this.

STARDUST
Given the fact that the Stardust and the Embassy were on on the same nights makes the Stardust's figures very impressive. Throughout 1974 their figures were steady, going from around the 700 mark to when sold-out signs went up on the door on

Thursday 19 December 1974 for a performance by Fran O'Toole and the Miami. Local showband Peter Boy and the Trend drew a crowd of 1,043 in December of the same year.

Some of the figures for the Stardust in 1974 were:

January 1974
Saturday 5 – Buckshot, 853
Saturday 12 – Philosophers, 700
Saturday 19 – Peter Boy and the Trend, 736
Saturday 26 – Some People, 753

May 1974
Saturday 3 – Scene Showband, 794
Saturday 10 – Boys and Girls, 871
Saturday 17 – Rascals, 851
Saturday 24 – Some People, 771

December 1974
Saturday 14 – Candy, 857
Thursday 19 – Fran O'Toole and the Miami, Sold Out
Saturday 28 – Peter Boy and the Trend, 1,043

Admission to all the above dances was 60p.

A large crowd enjoy a dance at the Embassy Ballroom in the 1960s.

Miami Showband Tragedy

On Wednesday 30 July 1975, Fran O'Toole and the Miami Showband were about to go on stage at the Castle Ballroom in Banbridge, County Down. Little did they know that this gig would be the last the Miami would play, or sadly the last day of three of the band members' lives. On their way home, their van was stopped at a bogus military checkpoint and three of the band members, Fran O'Toole, Brian McCoy and Tony Geraghty, were shot dead. Steven Travers was gravely wounded and only survived by pretending he was dead. Des Lee was blown over a ditch by the force of a bomb blast and was not critically injured. He was able to alert the RUC at their barracks in Newry after the gunmen had left the scene.

When the lead singer of a top band leaves, it normally signals the end of that band's career. However, it's fair to say this was not the case with the Miami Showband. Fran O'Toole had taken over as lead singer when the legendary Dickie Rock left the Miami to form his own band, and it has to be said he enjoyed almost

Fran O'Toole and the Miami Showband after Dickie Rock left to form his own band. They continued to draw large audiences throughout Ireland.

The Miami Showband, taken shortly before the fatal tragedy.

the same success as Dickie Rock had. He pulled in massive crowds the length and breadth of the country, appealing to the younger teenage dancers. Following the Miami massacre, Joe Dolan and a host of Irish showband stars refused to play in the North of Ireland for many years after. I read this saying somewhere and I think a lot of people would subscribe to the same sentiment: 'I'd walk a million miles for one of your smiles … Miami.'

A monument dedicated to the murdered Miami Showband members was unveiled on 10 December 2007 at Parnell Square in Dublin.

The Miami perform for their adoring fans.

The last Derry showband, the Foyle Showband. Included are Damien Godfrey, Robert Goodman, Stephen Bradley, Mickey Wilson, Jimmy McCullagh, Eddie Doherty, Richie McLaughlin and Christie Doherty.

The Foyle Showband: Last of an Era

The showband days were relived again for a while in Derry when the Foyle Showband was formed around 1997. This eight-piece band was very popular with the dancers of the Stardust and Du Pont halls. They performed regularly to sell-out crowds and played all over Ireland. To demonstrate how popular they were around the country, one gig springs to mind. At a private function in the Mount Errigal Hotel in Letterkenny, the band was booked to play from 11.00pm until 1.00am. When 1.00am came, the floor was packed with dancers all having a ball. The organiser of the function approached the band's manager and said they would give the band an extra £500 to play another thirty minutes. The boys agreed and duly played another half-hour. Back again came the organiser and repeated the offer for a further thirty minutes; again the boys in the band agreed. After further extended periods of playing, the band eventually left the stage, completely drained, at 4.00am! They were happy, although completely shattered, but with a bumper night's pay in their pockets.

This happened in a few other private functions down the country. However, with the musicians being in full-time employment and not getting home until 6.00am at times, it was inevitable that the travelling would take its toll eventually. This is exactly what happened in 2006 and the band disbanded that year. When they called it a day, it was ironic that the band's diary was full of bookings.

The Original Ballroom of Romance

The original, and without doubt the most famous, ballroom in Ireland was the Rainbow Ballroom of Romance situated at a crossroads in Glenfarne, County Leitrim. Built in 1934 by a local man, John McGivern, the ballroom gained world-wide recognition when a film was made about it and the people who danced and romanced there. The film received rave reviews and was screened in several countries. To this day, the old ballroom still attracts many visitors from every corner of Ireland, and indeed from Irish exiles throughout the globe. Dances are still held every third Sunday of each month and are attended by people from all over the country, many coming just to be able to say they danced in the famous ballroom of romance.

John McGivern was working in America in the 1930s when he decided to pack up his bags and return to Glenfarne. On his arrival back home, he decided to build a ballroom; local people thought he was mad to do this. Nevertheless, John, not a man easily dissuaded, went ahead with his dream and started building the ballroom in early 1934. It was a simple construction; just four block walls and a tin roof. It opened its doors in late 1934 and was an instant success with people coming from all parts to dance there.

The origin of the name Ballroom of Romance came from John's introduction of what was known as the romantic interlude. This was a fifteen-minute special appearance by John who would join the band on stage. Dressed in a black suit, white shirt and black bow tie, he would sing a few romantic songs. It was well known to the locals that his favourite song was *Have You Ever Been Lonely?* which he sang often.

*John McGivern outside his
beloved Ballroom of Romance.*

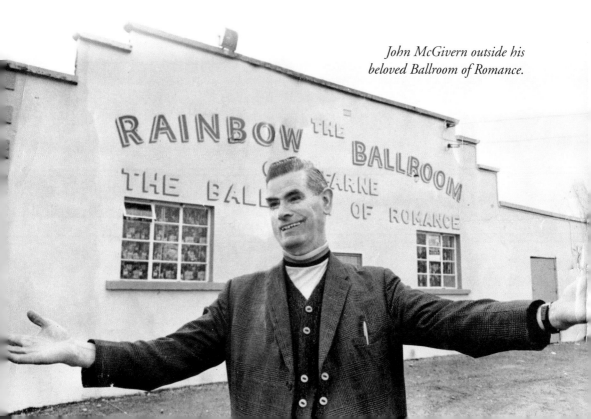

He wasn't a great singer but every inch a showman. When he got the couples onto the dance floor he would stop singing and encourage them to shake hands and introduce themselves to each other. When he finished his three romantic songs, he would suggest the boy take the girl up to the mineral bar for a lemonade. Many people actually met their wives or husbands through this procedure.

John would also announce from the stage, with the couple's approval, the engagement or the wedding date of some of the couples who met in the ballroom, and particularly during his romantic interlude. These announcements became folklore in this part of Ireland.

All the showbands throughout the country played at the Rainbow Ballroom of Romance. Arguably the most popular showband to play there was the Melody Aces from Newtownstewart in County Tyrone. The Gay McIntyre Showband and Willie Campbell Showband from Derry were also very popular.

John McGivern presenting his famous romantic interlude in the original Ballroom of Romance in Glenfarne, County Leitrim.

Gerry Finneran of the Glenfarne Community Development Trust, which has kept the ballroom alive for so many years, proudly told me:

'We are at present building an impressive archive, incorporating a museum commemorating the ballroom's great history. Busloads of people from all over Ireland still come to dance here. And it is fast becoming a cult tourist attraction.

'The showbands may be long gone, but we have no intention of giving up. We will keep on waltzing around Glenfarne's Rainbow Ballroom of Romance. And we invite dancers from everywhere to come and join us. The last waltz is not over yet!'

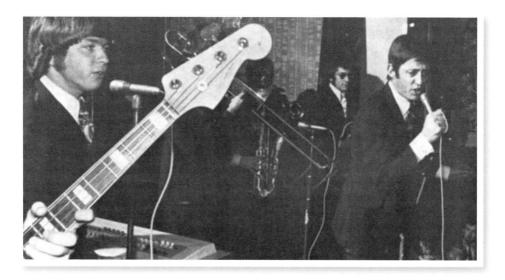

The legendary Dickie Rock and Fran O'Toole entertain the crowd as only they can.

The Big Five

Two of the 'Big Five' showband singers, although now in their twilight years, are still performing: Dickie Rock and Brendan Bowyer. They still, albeit on a limited scale, play some of the small theatres and the odd dinner dance. Arguably a little past their best, they are still capable of giving a performance that gives pleasure to people of a certain age. When they perform all the old favourites they still evoke a twinge of nostalgia. Some showband fans I have talked to expressed the opinion that they should hang up their mikes and go out at the top, as they preferred to remember them when they were at their best. Others, like me, contend that as people are still prepared to go and see them perform, admittedly in decreasing numbers, then why should they retire? Dickie Rock told me, 'I love performing on stage and I still get a great buzz out of seeing the audience enjoying themselves. If I ever go to a gig and don't enjoy it, then I will know it's time to call it a day. But that day is still a long way off.'

Dickie Rock is a true showband legend and his longevity in the business is testament to his overall popularity with the people who grew up during the Borderland, Stardust, Memorial Hall and Embassy heydays. People keep asking what age Dickie is. My response is simply why does it matter? He has taken care of himself through the years, he looks well, he sings well and he moves about the stage like a teenager, so the question of his age is irrelevant. He himself gets over the thorny question by simply saying, 'There is a certain mystique about a person's age and that's the way I prefer to keep it.'

Take a bow, Dickie, you sure deserve it.

Brendan Bowyer and the Royal Showband also contributed an enormous amount to the showband days as I have documented earlier. My knowledge of Brendan Bowyer is not plentiful, but he is the essence of professionalism on stage and is spoken of highly by everyone who has worked with him over the years. His top hit was *The Hucklebuck* and it is regarded as the anthem of the showband days. The Royal had a great line-up and a great camaraderie existed between them, as the band members never changed for years. Before, in Tom Dunphy, they had a talent that other showbands would have given their eyeteeth for. I have never heard anyone in the music industry say a bad word about the musicians that formed the Royal Showband and I think that sums the band up.

Our very own Johnny Quigley All Stars were at one time Ireland's top showband. People crowded into ballrooms everywhere to hear them play. They brought the American touch to the ballrooms of Ireland. They thrilled crowds from Derry to Cork and the memory of that great band is still vivid in people's minds to this day. How good were Johnny's All Stars? Well, when Brendan Bowyer was asked by Gerry Kelly on his UTV show who was the best showband of them all, Bowyer answered, 'It has to be the Johnny Quigley All Stars. They had so much talent on stage and every man could sing and sing well.' There is the answer, loud and clear, and who would dispute the opinion of a showband icon like Brendan Bowyer?

Along with the three notables mentioned could be added Joe Dolan and the Drifters. Joe was without doubt the biggest draw of any showband singer still performing, right up until his death. Whether it was in rural Ireland or the cities, he packed them in, and the people

absolutely loved him. He holds the record for drawing the biggest crowd to any dance hall in this part of Ireland. That says it all about Joe Dolan.

Strabane's Clipper Carlton lit the fuse and put the zip into the dance-hall scene at that time. They made a huge contribution to the entertainment of the Irish people, who still fondly remember their monologue, *Boot Hill*, and they rightly take their place as the band that started the phenomenon that was the Irish showbands.

All the showbands in Ireland in their own way contributed to the showband era. Each and every one of them gave their all on stage so that we could enjoy our nights at the dances. In music and entertainment terms, we had a lot back then, and for that we are thankful. Noel McBride sums up the days of the young people of the 1950s, '60s and '70s and the days of the showbands and dance halls of yesteryear with this nice little monologue entitled *Where Did The Good Times Go?*

Monday night was picture night, we got a few bob from the broo.
Heading off to the City picture house, great craic among the queue.
It didn't matter what was on, we queued up for the stalls.
We slagged the boys going in with girls with the fags and brandy balls.

The City, Palace, Strand, Rialto, Midland are all gone and also the Hall.
We had six picture houses back then when we were small.
Tuesday night was dancing night; it was always the same toot.
We washed our faces, put on a clean shirt and headed for the Crit.

When the last dance came, we were eyeing up the girls and all starry-eyed.
Then our pals came over and warned us, they're from the Waterside.
We had the Crit, Corinthian, Ashfield, Richmond, Borderland and the Mem.
Oh, aye, the Embassy and the Guildhall, I nearly forgot them.

I remember the Guildhall on a Friday night with the old tie and collar.
For Father McMonagle's supper dance, you had to pay a dollar.
We had great bands back then, Stan Cauley and the Blue Notes, Dickie McManus
and the Woodchoppers, Mick McWilliams and the Lakewood Swingtette.

Josie and Gay McIntyre and Johnny Quigley's one-night stand,
Betty and Kay, Jimmy Liddy, Hector and Willie Campbell's band.
Wednesday, where will we go tonight?
The shows? Naw, a dance? Naw, we used to argue and fight.

Snooker hall or up the town?
It was Wednesday night and we still had half-a-crown.

We made our minds up there and then, it's the Midland in the Waterside.
One and three for the stalls, and the same for ten Park Drive.

The show was rotten and they had no heat on, it was like a fridge.
We dandered home at eleven, into Cassoni's and over the bridge.
Thursday was D-Day and we went to the dole,
Only thing in my pocket was a great big hole.

That night I called round for Hooker,
Then off to the Minor Hall for a game of snooker.
Thursday night was the same, always chock-a-block,
I had to write my name on a board with a wee bit of chalk.

We mooched around for ninepence, we collected all the balls.
It was a popular game then with over a dozen snooker halls.
Remember Joe Zammit's, the Central, GOH Sports Club, Forrester's, Banks,
McMenamin's and the Star,
Cnoc na Ros and the Oxford Rooms where you didn't have to go far.

Friday night was a big night, you got thirty bob from your ma.
And you could stay out until two if it was all right with your da.
A dozen places you could go and we had plenty of funds.
Went to a dance and called to the bakery after that, and brought home a lot of buns.

Saturday morning and the big lay in, and after a feed of stews,
We'd all head off to the Brandywell to see Derry play the Blues.
Five o'clock, quick up the town to get the results of the match
From a big TV set in Cavendish's window, you could always stand and watch.

Back to the house, 'Ma, I need a clean shirt.'
'Why?' she asks, 'what's wrong with the one you had on last night, did the collar
get any dirt?'
'There's your tie, simmit and your pants.'
A quick look at the *Ireland's Saturday Night*, then it was off to the dance.

Sunday morning, it was out early at eight o'clock or nine.
Took the oul' dog out the Letterkenny Road, then on out the line.
Back to the house, a big bowl of soup and a quick cup of tea.
And we would all go down and see the big Yankee boats, sitting down the quay.

The versatility of the dancers is captured in this picture taken in the Plaza Ballroom in
1965. Some are twisting, some are waltzing and some are jiving – all to the same song!
The young twisters are getting some odd reactions from mature onlookers.

Sunday night, girls we will never forget, remember up the town.
We would walk Carlisle Road a hundred times, up, turn, down.

And all the fellows and girls chatting, and courting away in the dark.
Sure you were always disappointed if you never got off your mark.

Times have changed, to tell you the truth,
And you feel sorry today for all the Derry youth.
They have big centres, swimming pools and clubs and they're a great help I know.
But I hope someday they can turn and say, where did the good times go?

The Ballroom Days Come to an End

In the mid- to late 1960s, the showband era was at its peak and in full swing, with dances on an average of five nights a week. There were in excess of 500 showbands who toured the many ballrooms in every county in Ireland, employing around 4,000 musicians.

Fortunes were made and lost by many musicians who were brought from obscurity in low-paid jobs with an average weekly wage of £15 in the mid-'60s to being in the spotlight on stage and earning approximately £50 for a few nights' work. Most of the successful showbands were commanding fees of £600–£700 a night, but the five or six superstar showbands, like the Royal, Miami and Drifters, were commanding fees of around £1,000, which is equivalent to £8,000 in today's money. This was because the likes of the Big 3, Brendan Bowyer, Joe Dolan and Dickie Rock and their showbands were able to demand a percentage of the 'door' because they drew sell-out crowds everywhere they played. This arrangement would bring these particular showbands even more money.

A look at Jimmy Kelly's records on Borderland's bookings, crowd attendance and fees paid out to the bands confirms this. Certainly, the promoters were also making a fortune and many a showband manager told me the clergy were the worst promoters to deal with, as they were always crying poverty.

One thing was certain and undeniable – the dance-hall owners up and down the country were a short-sighted bunch. Surely their biggest mistake was not to reinvest some of the profits amassed from years of sell-out crowds at their venues back into the dance halls. Had they done so, and made the venues more comfortable for their patrons, it without doubt would have added years to the life of the dance-hall era. Not only did they *not* do that, they also refused to change with the times. For example, had they applied and fought hard enough for bar licences, this surely would have also help extend the showband years.

Normally, the dancers would leave the bars around 10.30pm in their droves to go to the dance halls just before the big showband came on stage. This fact was not lost on the bar owners, who were now thinking of ways of keeping the customers in their premises and were not slow to apply for, and be granted, late licences. They also started to book small bands to play in their bars. With this new development, people started to leave the bars at a much later time to go to the dances. With the ballrooms only offering tea, sandwiches and lemonade for sale, this made them less appealing to most people as times progressed.

Eventually, more and more customers didn't leave at all and just stayed in the bars instead of going to the ballrooms. The bars continued to heap pressure on the ballrooms when they laid small dance floors in their premises for their patrons. This really hastened the dance-halls' demise. Soon, every bar had a small dance floor and they were now booking two- three- and four-piece bands. Some went further and had a mainline cabaret star on the show. The Point Inn is a perfect example of this.

Showbands everywhere were now finding it very difficult to get bookings, as ballrooms were closing on a weekly basis all around the country. Showband musicians were soon out of work and had to adapt to the changing times. Most broke up and reformed into smaller groups, playing the pub circuit.

Within a space of two years, over 80% of the dance halls in the country had closed and those that remained were struggling to make ends meet. Borderland finally closed its doors after Teddy Palmer and his Rumble Band played there on Friday 18 February 1977. It was the end of a never-to-be-forgotten era in Irish entertainment.

It was a time when the dances were viewed as a social event.

It was a time when showbands gave their all on stage, playing only live music.

It was a time when dancers jived, waltzed and smooched all night long and cooled themselves off with the only refreshments on sale being tea or lemonade.

It was a time when the showbands' motto was 'send them home sweating'.

The last dance was over, the crowds had left and the dance halls were empty. All that was left was the echo of the last words spoken by the showband singer: 'Goodnight, God bless and safe home.' Outside the silent dance halls, the last remaining dancers took their seats on the waiting buses, cars and minibuses. Then, one by one, they rolled out of Ireland's cities and small villages for the last time. As the last bus pulled out, silence descended on the small but once-bustling villages. The showband and ballroom/dance-hall time had finally run its course.

All that are left now are the memories.

The Memory Makers

The Derry Showbands who gave us some great memories and provided so much pleasure to the dancers of Derry, Donegal, Tyrone and all over Ireland included:

The Bankers
The Barristers
The Beaumont 7
The Blue Notes
The Willie Campbell Showband
The Capri
The Carlton Swingtette
The Stan Cauley Orchestra
The Checkers
The Cheries
The Clipper Carlton (Strabane)
The Coasters
The Crescent
The Derry City Showband
The Derrytones Showband
The Dynachords
The Embassy Orchestra
The Emperors
The Esquires
The Flingels
The Foyle Showband
The Friends
The Golden Seven

The Imperial All Stars
Johnny and the Jokers
The Kingston All Stars
The Lakewood Swingtette
The Magnificent Seven
The Mainliners
Gay McIntyre Showband
Josie McIntyre Band
The Melody Makers
The Olympic All Stars
The Johnny Quigley All Stars
The Rising Sons Showband
The Saints Showband
The Signetts
The Statesiders Showband
The Swing Aces
The Swingtones
The Tahiti Showband
The Trade Winds (folk group)
Peter Boy and the Trend
The Woodchoppers
The Woodlanders

compliments
Johnny Quigley ALL STARS and Neil J. Gier
DERRY

242